W

This book is due for return on or before the last date shown
above; it may, subject to the book not being reserved by
another reader, be renewed by personal application, post, or
telephone, quoting this date and details of the book.

HAMPSHIRE COUNTY LIBRARY

X

D1423261

STAR TALES

Orion, the giant hunter, stands in front of his constellation (Lilika Papanicolaou).

STAR TALES

Ian Ridpath

Lutterworth Press
Cambridge

Lutterworth Press
P.O. Box 60
Cambridge CB1 2NT

British Library Cataloguing in Publication Data
Ridpath, Ian
 Star tales.
 1. Ancient civilizations. Astronomy.
 Theories
 I. Title
 521'.5'093

 ISBN 0-7188-2695-7

First published in the UK 1988 by Lutterworth Press

Printed in the United States of America

CONTENTS

—*Preface*—

Storytelling is one of the most engaging of human arts, and what greater inspiration to a storyteller's imagination than the stars of night. This book of star tales has its roots in a series of skywatching guides that I produced in conjunction with the great Dutch celestial cartographer Wil Tirion. As I came to describe each constellation, I found myself wondering about its origin and the way in which ancient people had personified it in mythology. Astronomy books did not contain satisfactory answers; they either gave no mythology at all, or they recounted stories that, I later discovered, were not true to the Greek originals. I decided, therefore to write my own book on the mythology of the constellations and a fascinating undertaking it proved to be.

My theme has been how Greek and Roman literature has shaped our perception of the constellations as we know them today – for, surprisingly enough, the constellations recognized by twentieth century science are primarily those of the ancient Greeks, interspersed with modern additions. To this end, I have gone back to original Greek and Latin sources wherever possible; references are given at the end of the book. While I have attempted to recount the main variants of each myth, and to identify the writer concerned where appropriate, it should be realized that there is no such thing as a 'correct' myth; for some stories, there are almost as many different versions as there are mythologists.

I should also make clear what this book is not about: I have not tried to compare the Greek and Roman constellations with the constellations that were imagined by other cultures such as the Egyptian, Hindu or Chinese. Fascinating though the differences are, such a diversion would, I think, have taken me too far from my intended task. Neither have I delved too far into the confusing morass of speculation about the origin of the constellations; that is a job for the historian, and indeed we may never be able to provide convincing answers from the fragmentary information available.

Since ancient astronomers regarded each constellation as embodying a picture of a mythological character or an animal, rather than as simply an area of sky as defined by today's surveyor-astronomers, it seemed natural to illustrate each constellation with a picture from an old star map. These star maps are works of art in themselves, and are among the most elegant treasures bequeathed to us by astronomers of the past. The constellations give us a very real link with the most ancient civilizations. It is a heritage that we can share whenever we look at the night sky.

I am indebted to many people for their assistance in the preparation of this book. The expertise of David Dewhirst at the University of Cambridge proved invaluable in tracking down some obscure references. My research was further aided by the help and interest of Janet Dudley and John Hutchins at the Royal Greenwich Observatory library, and Peter Hingley at the Royal Astronomical Society library. I owe a particular debt of gratitude to David Calvert at the Royal Greenwich Observatory for supplying the constellation illustrations, photographed from the star atlases of Bode and Flamsteed preserved in the Observatory's library. I gratefully acknowledge the assistance of George and Lena Bekerman with translation from the French. Wil Tirion provided help with information on the Dutch constellation-makers Keyser and de Houtman. John Ebdon, director of the London Planetarium, who is as ardent a Graecophile as he is an astronomer, most kindly read my manuscript and suggested some improvements. It is also a pleasure to thank the Greek artist Lilika Papanicolaou for permission to reproduce the frontispiece.

—*Stars and storytellers*—

EVERY NIGHT, A PAGEANT OF GREEK MYTHOLOGY CIRCLES OVERHEAD. PERSEUS FLIES TO THE RESCUE OF ANDROMEDA, ORION FACES THE charge of the snorting bull, Boötes herds the bears around the pole, and the ship of the Argonauts sails in search of the golden fleece. These legends, along with many others, are depicted in the star patterns that astronomers term constellations.

Constellations are the invention of human imagination, not of nature. They are an expression of the human desire to impress its own order upon the apparent chaos of the night sky. For navigators beyond sight of land or for travellers in the trackless desert who wanted signposts, for farmers who wanted a calendar and for shepherds who wanted a nightly clock, the division of the sky into recognizable star groupings had practical purposes. But perhaps the earliest motivation was to humanize the forbidding blackness of night.

Newcomers to astronomy are soon disappointed to find that the great majority of constellations bear little, if any, resemblance to the figures whose names they carry; but to expect such a resemblance is to misunderstand their true meaning. The constellation figures are not intended to be taken literally. Rather, they are symbolic, a celestial allegory. The night sky was a screen on which human imagination could project the deeds and personifications of deities, sacred animals and moral tales. It was a picture book in the days before writing.

Each evening, the stars emerge like magic spirits as the Sun descends to its nocturnal lair. Twentieth-century science has told us that those twinkling points scattered across the sky in their thousands are actually glowing balls of gas similar to our own Sun, immensely far away. A star's brightness in the night sky is a combination of its own power output and its distance from us. So far apart are the stars that light from even the nearest of them takes many years to reach us. The human eye, detecting the faint spark from star fires, is seeing across unimaginable gulfs of both space and time.

Such facts were unknown to the ancient Greeks and their predecessors, to whom we owe the constellation patterns that we recognize today. They were not aware that, with a few exceptions, the stars of a constellation have no connection with each other, but lie at widely differing distances. Chance alone has given us such familiar shapes as the 'W' of Cassiopeia, the square of Pegasus, the sickle of Leo or the Southern Cross.

The constellation system that we use today has grown from a list of forty-eight constellations published around AD 150 by the Greek scientist Ptolemy in an influential book called the *Almagest*. Since then, various astronomers have added another forty constellations, filling the gaps between Ptolemy's figures and populating the region around the south celestial pole that was below the horizon of the Greeks. The result is a total of eighty-eight constellations that all astronomers accept by international agreement. The tales of these constellations are told in this book – along with nearly two dozen others that fell by the wayside.

Ptolemy did not invent the constellations that he listed. They are much older than his era, though exactly when and where the constellations were invented is lost in the mists of time. The early Greek writers Homer and Hesiod (*c.* 700 BC) mentioned only a few star groups, such as the Great Bear, Orion and the Pleiades star cluster (the Pleiades was then regarded as a separate constellation rather than being incorporated in Taurus as today).

The major developments evidently took place farther east, around the Tigris and Euphrates rivers in what is now Iraq. There lived the Babylonians, who at the time of Homer and Hesiod had a well-established system of constellations of the zodiac, the strip of sky traversed liy the Sun, Moon and planets. We know this from a star list written in cuneiform on a clay tablet dated to around 700 BC. Scholars call this list the *mul-Apin* series, from the first name recorded on the tablet. The Babylonian constellations had many similarities with those we know today, but they are not all identical. From other texts, historians have established that the constellations known to the Babylonians actually originated much earlier, with their ancestors the Sumerians before 2000 BC.

If the Greeks of Homer and Hesiod's day knew of the Babylonian zodiac they did not write about it. The first clear evidence we have for an extensive set of Greek constellations comes from the astronomer Eudoxus (*c.*390–*c.*340 BC). Eudoxus reputedly learned the constellations from priests in Egypt and introduced them to Greece, which makes his contribution to astronomy highly significant. He published descriptions of the constellations in two works called *Enoptron* (*Mirror*) and *Phaenomena* (*Appearances*). Both these works are lost, but the *Phaenomena* lives on in a poem of the same name by another Greek, Aratus (*c.*315–*c.*245 BC). Aratus's *Phaenomena* gives us a complete guide to the constellations known to the ancient Greeks; hence he is a major figure in our study of constellation lore.

Aratus was born at Soli in Cilicia, on the southern coast of what is now Turkey. He studied in Athens before going to the court of King Antigonus of Macedonia in northern Greece. There, at the king's request, he produced his poetic version of the *Phaenomena* of Eudoxus around 275 BC. In the *Phaenomena* Aratus identified forty-seven constellations, including the Water (now regarded as part of Aquarius) and the Pleiades. Aratus also named six individual stars: Arcturus, Capella (which he called Aix), Sirius,

Procyon (which formed a constellation on its own), Spica (which he called Stachus) and Vindemiatrix (which he called Protrygeter). This last star is a surprise, since it is so much fainter than the others, but the Greeks used it as a calendar star since its rising at dawn in August marked the start of the grape harvest.

Neither the Greeks nor the Egyptians actually invented the constellations that are described in the *Phaenomena*. The evidence for that statement lies not just in written records, but in the sky itself.

Surprisingly, it is not too difficult to work out roughly where and when the constellations known to Eudoxus and Aratus were invented. The clue is that Aratus described no constellations around the south celestial pole, for the reason that this area of sky was permanently below the horizon of the constellation-makers. Since the constellation-free zone has a radius of about 36 degrees, the constellation makers must have lived at a latitude of about 36 degrees north – that is, south of Greece but north of Egypt.

A second clue comes from the fact that the constellation-free zone is centred not on the south celestial pole at the time of Aratus but on its position over 1500 years before him, at a date of about 2000 BC. (The position of the celestial pole changes slowly with time because of a wobble of the Earth on its axis, an effect known as precession.) Therefore we can conclude that the constellations described by Aratus were invented around 2000 BC by people who lived close to latitude 36 degrees north.

This date is too early for the Greeks and the latitude is too far south; Egyptian civilization is sufficiently old, but the required latitude is well north of them. The time and the place, though, ideally match the Babylonians and their Sumerian ancestors who, as we have already seen, had a well-developed knowledge of astronomy by 2000 BC. Hence two independent lines of evidence point to the Babylonians and Sumerians as the originators of our constellation system.

But why had the constellation system introduced by Eudoxus not been updated by its makers to take account of the changing position of the celestial pole? As we have seen, the constellations introduced by Eudoxus and described by Aratus in the *Phaenomena* refer to the position of the celestial pole over 1500 years earlier. By the time of Aratus, the shift in position of the celestial pole meant that certain stars mentioned in the *Phaenomena* were now permanently below the horizon from latitude 36 degrees north, while others not mentioned by Aratus had by then come into view. Oddly, Eudoxus himself seems not to have been bothered by these anomalies, if he even noticed them; but the great Greek astronomer Hipparchus (*fl.*146–127 BC) recognized the differences and was understandably critical.

A new twist to the tale of the constellations has been added by Professor Archie Roy of Glasgow University, who has argued that the Babylonian constellations must have reached Egypt (and hence Eudoxus) via some other civilization; he proposes the Minoans of Crete. Professor Roy notes that the *Phaenomena* of Aratus embodies much nautical weather lore

The forty-eight constellations of the Greek astronomer Ptolemy, illustrated on a pair of woodcuts made by Albrecht Dürer in 1515, one showing the northen sky (left) and the other the southern sky (right). The figures are shown from the rear, as on a celestial globe.

associated with the appearance of various star groups. Professor Roy interprets this as evidence that the constellations were intended as a navigational aid for seamen.

Accurate knowledge of the sky would have been vital to navigators, who would set their course at night from the rising and setting points of various stars and constellations. These seafarers could have been completely different people from the constellation makers. Professor Roy concludes that the seafarers concerned were the Minoans who lived on Crete and the surrounding islands off the coast of Greece, including Thera (also known as Santorini). Crete lies between 35 and 36 degrees north, which is the right latitude, and the Minoan empire was expanding between 3000 and 2000 BC. which is the right date.

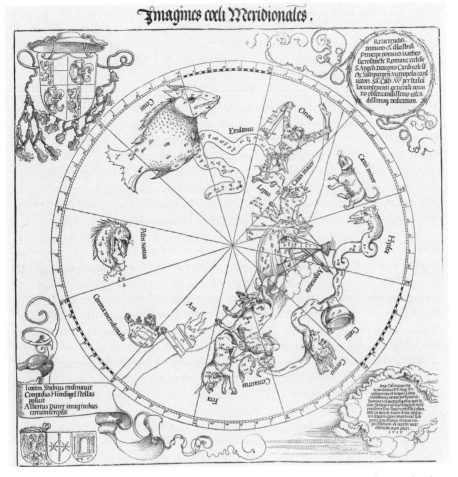

Note the large blank area in the southern sky that was below the horizon to the people who invented the constellations. The size of this blank zone is a clue to the latitude at which the constellation inventors lived. (The National Maritime Museum, London).

What's more, the Minoans were in contact with the Babylonians through Syria from an early stage. Hence they must have been familiar with the old Babylonian constellations, and they could well have adapted the Babylonian star groups into a practical system for navigation.

But the Minoan civilization was wiped out in 1450 BC by the explosive eruption of a volcano on the island of Thera about 120 km north of Crete. It was one of the greatest natural catastrophes in the history of civilization, the probable origin of the legend of Atlantis. Professor Roy supposes that Minoan refugees brought their knowledge of the stars to Egypt after the eruption, where it was eventually encountered by Eudoxus in unchanged form over 1000 years later.

During the writing of this book I visited Crete. The stars hang lower there; you feel that you could strip them from the sky in handfuls like grapes from a vine. The Milky Way arches overhead like a tangled skein of phosphorescent wool. As the Earth turns you cannot fail to notice stars gradually sink into the placid sea on one horizon while others emerge from the deep on the other horizon.

Professor Roy's thesis is an attractive one, for it is easy to imagine the Minoans utilizing the Babylonian constellation system in the way that he describes. In addition, many star myths are centred on Crete. In the face of Mount Dikte overlooking the Lassithi plateau is the cave where the infant Zeus, king of the Greek gods, was reputedly reared. However, it must be admitted that there is no direct evidence, such as wall paintings or star lists like those of the Babylonians, to demonstrate any Minoan interest in astronomy. So, for now, the theory that the Minoans were middlemen to our constellation system remains nothing more than an appealing idea.

The *Phaenomena* of Aratus was an immensely popular poem and was later translated several times into Latin. For our purposes the most useful version is a Latin adaptation of Aratus attributed to Germanicus Caesar (15 BC–AD 19), since it has more information about the identification of certain constellations than Aratus's original. According to the scholar D.B. Gain this Latin version of the *Phaenomena* could have been written either by Germanicus or by his uncle (and adoptive father) Tiberius Caesar, but in this book I refer to the authorsimply as Germanicus.

After Aratus, the next landmark in our study of Greek constellation lore is Eratosthenes (*c.*276–*c.*194 BC), to whom an essay called the *Catasterisms* is attributed. Eratosthenes was a Greek scientist and writer who worked in Alexandria at the mouth of the Nile. The *Catasterisms* gives the mythology of forty-two separate constellations (the Pleiades cluster is treated individually), with a listing of the main stars in each figure. The version of the *Catasterisms* that survives is only a summary of the original, made at some unknown date, and it is not even certain that the original was written by the real Eratosthenes; hence the author of the *Catasterisms* is usually referred to as pseudo-Eratosthenes. The antiquity of his sources is certain, though, because he quotes in places from a long-lost work on astronomy by Hesiod (*c.*700 BC).

Another influential source of constellation mythology is a book called *Poetic Astronomy* by a Roman author named Hyginus, apparently written in the second century AD. We do not know who Hyginus was, not even his full name – he was evidently not C. Julius Hyginus, a Roman writer of the first century BC. *Poetic Astronomy* is based on the constellations listed by Eratosthenes (Hyginus differs only by including the Pleiades under Taurus), but it contains many additional stories. Hyginus also wrote a compendium of general mythology called the *Fabulae*. In medieval and Renaissance times many illustrated versions of Hyginus's writings on astronomy were produced.

Marcus Manilius, a Roman author of whom virtually nothing is known, wrote a book called *Astronomica* around the year AD 15, clearly influenced by the *Phaenomena* of Aratus. Manilius's book deals mostly with astrology rather than astronomy, but it contains numerous insights into constellation lore and I have quoted him a number of times.

The names of three other mythologists appear frequently on the pages that follow, and although they are not astronomers they must be introduced before we return to the history of the constellations. Foremost among them is the Roman poet Ovid (43 BC–AD 17), who recounts many famous myths in his books the *Metamorphoses*, which deals with tranformations of all kinds, and the *Fasti*, a treatise on the Roman calendar. Apollodorus was a Greek who compiled an almost encyclopedic summary of myths some time in the late first century BC or in the first century AD. Finally there is the Greek writer Apollonius Rhodius (Apollonius of Rhodes) whose *Argonautica*, an epic poem on the voyage of Jason and the Argonauts composed in the third century BC, includes much mythological information. These are the main sources for the stories in this book.

Greek astronomy reached its pinnacle with Ptolemy (*c.* AD 100-*c.* 178) who worked in Alexandria, Egypt. Around AD 150, Ptolemy produced a summary of Greek astronomical knowledge usually known by its Arabic title of the *Almagest*. At its heart was a catalogue of 1022 stars arranged into forty-eight constellations (see table), with estimates of their brightness, which based largely on the observations of the Greek astronomer Hipparchus three centuries earlier.

The forty-eight constellations listed by the Greek astronomer Ptolemy in the second century AD

Andromeda	Cepheus	Lupus
Aquarius	Cetus	Lyra
Aquila	Corona Australis	Ophiuchus
Ara	Corona Borealis	Orion
Argo Navis (now	Corvus	Pegasus
subdivided into Carina,	Crater	Perseus
Puppis, Pyxis and	Cygnus	Pisces
Vela)	Delphinus	Piscis Austrinus
Aries	Draco	Sagitta
Auriga	Equuleus	Sagittarius
Boötes	Eridanus	Scorpius
Cancer	Gemini	Serpens
Canis Major	Hercules	Taurus
Canis Minor	Hydra	Triangulum
Capricornus	Leo	Ursa Major
Cassiopeia	Lepus	Ursa Minor
Centaurus	Libra	Virgo

Ptolemy did not identify the stars in his catalogue in Greek letters, as astronomers do today, but described their position within each constellation figure. For instance, Ptolemy's 'the reddish one on the southern eye' refers to the star in Taurus that we know today as Aldebaran. At times, this system became cumbersome: 'The northernmost of the two stars close together over the little shield in the poop' is how Ptolemy struggled to identify a star (now called Xi Puppis) in the obsolete constellation of Argo.

The tradition of describing stars by their positions within a constellation figure had already been established by Eratosthenes and Hipparchus. Clearly, the Greeks regarded the constellations not merely as assemblages of stars but as true pictures in the sky. Identifications would have been easier if they had given the stars individual names, but Ptolemy added only four stars to those named by Aratus four centuries earlier: Altair (which Ptolemy called Aetus, meaning eagle); Antares; Regulus (which he called Basiliscus); and Vega (which he called Lyra, the same name as its constellation).

It would be difficult to over-emphasize the influence of Ptolemy on astronomy; the constellation system we use today is essentially Ptolemy's, modified and extended. Mapmakers in Europe and Arabia used his constellation figures for over 1500 years, witness this passage from the preface to the *Atlas Coelestis* by the first Astronomer Royal, John Flamsteed, published in 1729:

> From Ptolemy's time to ours the names that he made use of have been continued by the ingenious and learned men of all nations; the Arabians always used his forms and names of the constellations; the old Latin catalogues of the fixed stars use the same; Copernicus's catalogue and Tycho Brahe's use the same; so do the catalogues published in the German, Italian, Spanish, Portuguese, French and English languages. All the observations of the ancients and moderns make use of Ptolemy's forms of the constellations and names of the stars so that there is a necessity of adhering to them, that we may not render the old observations unintelligible by altering or departing from them.

After Ptolemy, Greek astronomy went into permanent eclipse. By the eighth century AD the centre of astronomy had moved east from Alexandria to Baghdad where Ptolemy's work was translated into Arabic and received its name the *Almagest*. Al-Sufi (AD 903–86), one of the greatest Arabic astronomers (also known as Azophi), produced his own version of the *Almagest* called the *Book of the Fixed Stars* in which he introduced many star names.

According to Paul Kunitzsch, the German authority on Arabic star names, bedouin Arabs had their own names for various bright stars such as Aldebaran and they commonly regarded single stars as representing animals or people. For example, the stars we know as Alpha and Beta Ophiuchi were regarded by the Arabs as a shepherd and his dog, while neighbouring stars made up the outlines of a field with sheep. Some of the Arabic names were already so many centuries old that their meanings were lost even to al-Sufi and his contemporaries, and they remain unknown today. Other star names used by al-Sufi and his compatriots were direct translations of

Ptolemy's descriptions. For example, the star name Fomalhaut comes from the Arabic meaning 'mouth of the southern fish', which is where Ptolemy had described it in the *Almagest*.

From the tenth century onwards, the works of Ptolemy were reintroduced into Europe by Islamic Arab incursions and the Greek books were translated from Arabic into Latin, the scientific language of the day. Through this roundabout route we have obtained a polyglot system of Greek constellations with Latin names containing stars with Arabic titles.

Although the Arabs increased the number of star names, the number of constellations remained unchanged. The first extension of Ptolemy's forty-eight was made in 1551 on a celestial globe by the great Dutch cartographer Gerardus Mercator who depicted Antinous and Coma Berenices as separate constellations; in the *Almagest*, Ptolemy had mentioned these groups as sub-divisions of Aquila and Leo respectively. Following Mercator's lead, the great Danish astronomer Tycho Brahe listed Antinous and Coma Berenices separately in his influential star catalogue of 1602. Coma Berenices is still a recognized constellation, but Antinous has since been abandoned.

By now the age of exploration was well under way, and navigator-astronomers turned their attention to the hitherto uncharted regions of the sky in the southern hemisphere that had been below the horizon for the ancient Greeks. Three names stand out from this era: Petrus Plancius (1552–1622), a Dutch theologian and cartographer, and two Dutch navigators: Pieter Dirkszoon Keyser (also known as Petrus Theodorus or Peter Theodore) and Frederick de Houtman. Surprisingly, all three are little-known today despite their lasting contributions.

Plancius instructed Keyser to make observations to fill in the constellation-free zone around the south celestial pole. Keyser was chief pilot on the *Hollandia* and later on the *Mauritius*, two of the fleet of four ships that left the Netherlands in 1595 on the first Dutch trading expedition to the East Indies, sailing via Madagascar. Keyser was adept at astronomy and mathematics; the Dutch author A.J.M. Wanders, in his book *In the Realm of the Sun and Stars*, writes that Keyser observed from the crow's nest with an instrument given to him by Plancius. Keyser died in September 1596 while the fleet was at Bantam (now Banten, near the modern Serang in western Java). His catalogue of 135 stars, divided into twelve newly invented constellations, was delivered to Plancius when the fleet returned to Holland the following year. Regrettably, little else seems to be known about the life and accomplishments of Keyser, but he left his mark indelibly on the sky.

Keyser's twelve new constellations first appeared on a globe by Plancius in 1598, and again two years later on a globe by the Dutch cartographer Jodocus Hondius. Their acceptance was assured when Johann Bayer, a German astronomer, included them in his *Uranometria* of 1603, the leading star atlas of its day. Keyser's observations were published in tabular form by Johannes Kepler in the *Rudolphine Tables* of 1627.

The Dutch fleet in which Keyser sailed was commanded by the explorer

Cornelis de Houtman; among the crew was his younger brother Frederick de Houtman (1571–1627) who apparently assisted Keyser in his observations. On a second expedition in 1598 Cornelis was killed and Frederick was imprisoned by the Sultan of Atjeh in northern Sumatra. Frederick made good use of his two years in prison by studying the local Malay language and making astronomical observations.

In 1603, following his return to Holland, Frederick de Houtman published his observations as an appendix to a Malayan and Madagascan dictionary that he compiled, one of the most unlikely pieces of astronomical publishing in history. In the Introduction he wrote: 'Also added are the declinations of many fixed stars around the south pole; never seen before today. Observed and written down by Frederick de Houtman from Gouda.'

De Houtman increased Keyser's 135 measured star positions to 303, although 107 of these were stars already known to Ptolemy according to a study of the catalogue by the English astronomer E.B. Knobel. Nowhere did de Houtman give Keyser credit for his priority. De Houtman's catalogue of southern stars, divided into the same twelve constellations as those of Keyser, was used by the Dutch cartographer Willem Janszoon Blaeu for his celestial globes from 1603 onwards. Keyser and de Houtman are now credited jointly with the invention of these twelve southern constellations, which are still recognized today (see below).

Twelve constellations introduced 1596–1603 by Pieter Dirkszoon Keyser and Frederick de Houtman

Apus	Grus	**Musca**	Triangulum Australe
Chamaeleon	Hydrus	**Pavo**	Tucana
Dorado	Indus	**Phoenix**	Volans

As the accuracy of astronomical observations improved and fainter stars were charted, the opportunities grew for innovators to introduce new constellations even among the area of sky known to the ancient Greeks. In addition to charting the southern constellations of Keyser and de Houtman, Petrus Plancius invented some constellations of his own, among them Columba, the dove, which he formed from nine stars that Ptolemy had listed as surrounding Canis Major; he also invented the unlikely sounding Monoceros, the unicorn, and Camelopardalis, the giraffe, from faint stars uncharted by Ptolemy. These three Plancius constellations are still accepted by astronomers, but his other inventions fell by the wayside (see Chapter Four).

Eleven more constellations were introduced later in the seventeenth century by the Polish astronomer Johannes Hevelius (1611–87), filling the remaining gaps in the northern sky. They were illustrated in his star atlas called *Firmamentum Sobiescianum*, published posthumously in 1690. Oddly enough, Hevelius insisted on observing with the naked eye even though telescopes were by then available; many of his constellations were deliberately faint as though he was boasting of the power of his eyesight. Of

Hevelius's inventions, seven are still accepted by astronomers (see below). The rejected four were Cerberus, Mons Maenalus, Musca and Triangulum Minor.

Seven constellations introduced by Johannes Hevelius on his star map published posthumously in 1690

Canes Venatici	Leo Minor	**Scutum**	Vulpecula
Lacerta	Lynx	**Sextans**	

Although the northern constellations were now complete, there were still gaps in the southern sky. These were filled by the French astronomer Nicolas Louis de Lacaille (1713–62) who sailed to South Africa in 1750 and set up a small observatory at Cape Town under the famous Table Mountain, which impressed him so much that he later named a constellation after it, Mensa. At the Cape from August 1751 to July 1752 Lacaille observed the positions of nearly 10,000 stars, an astounding total in the short time.

On his return to France in 1754, Lacaille presented a map of the southern skies to the French Royal Academy of Sciences, including fourteen new constellations of his own invention (see below). The map was published in 1756, and Lacaille's new constellations were rapidly accepted by other astronomers.

Whereas Keyser and Houtman had mostly named their constellations after exotic animals, Lacaille commemorated instruments of science and art, with the exception of Mensa, named after the Table Mountain under which he had carried out his observations. His full catalogue, and a revised map, was published under the title *Coelum Australe Stelliferum* in 1763. In this catalogue, Lacaille divided up the unwieldy constellation Argo Navis, the ship, into the subsections Carina, Puppis and Vela that astronomers still use as separate constellations. As well as creating fourteen new constellations, Lacaille eliminated a pre-existing one – Robur Carolinum, Charles's Oak, introduced by the Englishman Edmond Halley in 1678 to honour King Charles II.

Fourteen constellations introduced by Nicolas Louis de Lacaille in 1754

Antlia	Fornax	Microscopium	Pictor	Sculptor
Caelum	Horologium	Norma	Pyxis	Telescopium
Circinus	Mensa	Octans	Reticulum	

All those from Lacaille's time onwards who gerrymandered with the constellations did so without lasting success, but there were plenty of astronomers who tried to leave their mark on the sky. Constellation mania had reached its height by 1801 when the German astronomer Johann Elert Bode (1747–1826) published his immense star atlas, *Uranographia*, containing over 100 different constellations; but by then astronomers realized that things had gone too far, and during the ensuing century this number was eroded by a process of natural wastage. In 1899 the American historian R.H. Allen summed up the prevailing situation in his book *Star Names and*

Their Meaning: 'From 80 to 90 constellations may be considered as now more or less acknowledged.'

One serious deficiency was that there were still no generally agreed boundaries to the constellations. Since Bode's time cartographers had shown dotted lines snaking between constellation figures, but these were arbitrary lines of demarcation that varied from atlas to atlas. The matter was settled once and for all by astronomy's governing body, the International Astronomical Union.

At its first General Assembly in 1922, the IAU officially adopted the list of eighty-eight constellations, covering the entire sky, that we use today. On behalf of the IAU a Belgian astronomer, Eugene Delporte (1882–1955), then drew up a definitive list of boundaries for these eighty-eight constellations. Delporte's work, published in 1930 in a book called *Délimitation Scientifique des Constellations*, amounts to an international treaty on the demarcation of the sky, which astronomers throughout the world have conformed to ever since. Constellations are now regarded not as star patterns but as precisely defined areas of sky, rather like countries on Earth. Unlike the map of the Earth, though, the map of the sky is unlikely to change.

Official boundaries to the constellations were fixed in 1930 by a Belgian astronomer, Eugene Delporte, acting on behalf of the International Astronomical Union. Here is his chart for part of the northern sky, including Cassiopeia and Andromeda. The constellation boundaries follow circles of right ascension (the equivalent of longitude in the sky) and parallels of declination (the celestial equivalent of latitude). (Royal Astronomical Society Library)

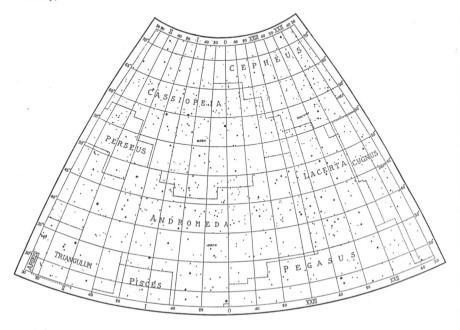

—*Star maps*—

EVERYONE IS FAMILIAR WITH MAPS OF THE EARTH, BUT TO MOST
PEOPLE A MAP OF THE SKY IS A MYSTERY. YET THERE ARE MANY
similarities because the celestial cartographer faces the same
problem as the terrestrial one: how to represent a curved surface on a flat
sheet.

The earliest representations of the sky were actually globes, on which the
constellations were shown as though viewed from a God-like position
beyond the stars; this meant that the constellation shapes were represented
back to front by comparison with the way we see them from Earth. In the
Museo Nazionale, Naples, is a marble statue of Atlas holding on his
shoulders a globe of the heavens on which the constellations are depicted in
this way. The sculpture is called the Farnese Atlas, after Cardinal
Alessandro Farnese (later Pope Paul III) who acquired it in the early
sixteenth century and exhibited it in the Farnese Palace in Rome. It is the
oldest known celestial globe, for historians think that the sculpture was
probably made in Rome around the second century AD. Even more
significantly, it is thought to be a copy of a Greek original from the third
century BC, the time at which Aratus wrote his *Phaenomena*. Thus the globe
held by the Farnese Atlas provides our only firsthand look at the star
pictures that the ancient Greeks imagined in the sky.

An early form of flat star chart was the astrolabe, popular with the
medieval Arabs. Usually made of brass, the astrolabe was a disk on which
the positions of bright stars were depicted for navigation purposes; the
principle lives on in the star-finding devices called planispheres used by
present-day amateur astronomers and sailors. The earliest surviving
astrolabes date from the ninth century AD, but written evidence shows that
they were known much earlier, possibly even in the time of Ptolemy, *c.*AD
150. Other than astrolabes, the oldest known flat sky map is a Chinese
drawing of *c.*AD 940 called the Tunhuang manuscript after the place at which
it was found; it is now in the British Museum.

Since the Tunhuang chart depicts the Chinese constellation tradition,
which was independent of that in Europe and Arabia, most of the
constellations are unrecognizable. Chinese constellations were smaller than
Western ones, and hence more numerous, each constellation usually

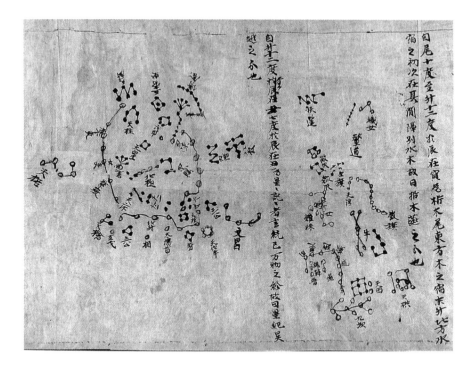

Chinese constellations differed markedly from western ones, being usually much smaller and using many of the fainter stars. This illustration shows a section of the northern sky from a chart believed to date from AD 940 that was found at Tunhuang (now Dunhuang), north central China. Among the Chinese constellations shown, only the familiar shape of the Plough or Big Dipper is recognizable. The Tunhuang manuscript is the oldest surviving star map in the world. (By permission of the British Library (MS Stein 3326).

consisting of only a handful of stars. Chinese astronomy was flourishing as far back as 240 BC, when they observed Halley's Comet. By the end of the third century AD, Chinese astronomers had developed a system of 283 constellations consisting of 1464 stars. These constellations did not depict myths but facets of Chinese life, such as *Ti-wang*, the emperor; *Shang-shu*, the secretaries; and *Huan-che*, the court eunuchs. This system was still in use when Jesuit missionaries introduced Western constellations to the Chinese in the seventeenth century.

Albrecht Dürer, the great German artist, produced the first notable European flat chart of the heavens in 1515; it was a pair of woodcuts, one showing the zodiac and all constellations north of it, the other showing all known constellations south of the zodiac, based on the stars and constellations catalogued by the Greek astronomer Ptolemy in his *Almagest*. In the four corners of the northern chart are stylized portraits of the four authorities whom Dürer used: Aratus, Ptolemy, Manilius and Azophi

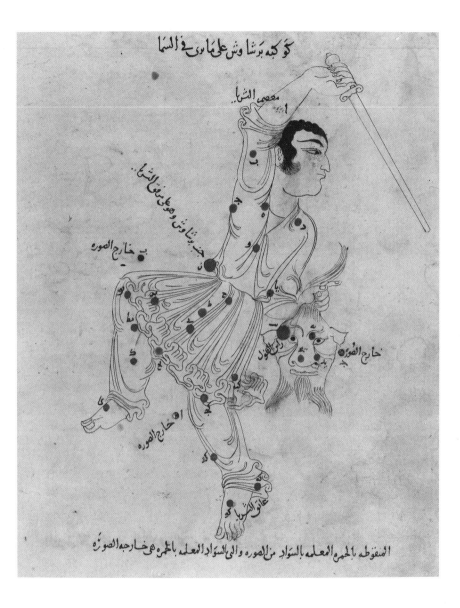

An Arabic representation of Perseus, from a version of the *Book of the Fixed Stars* by the Arabic astronomer al-Sufi. This particular manuscript was written and illustrated *c.* AD 1009, shortly after the death of al-Sufi himself. The manuscript contains two illustrations of each constellation, showing it as it appeared in the sky and also in reverse, as it would appear on a star globe; this plate shows Perseus as he appears in the sky. Perseus wears Arabic dress, and the head of Medusa the Gorgon has been depicted as a bearded male. The dotted object in the sword arm of Perseus depicts a twin cluster of stars known to modern astronomers as the Double Cluster. (By permission of the Bodleian Library (MS Marsh 144, p. 111).

(al-Sufi). The southerly map of the pair clearly shows the constellation-free zone around the south pole. Dürer depicted the constellations back to front, as on a celestial globe, a tradition that most early maps were to follow.

Star maps improved as astronomers surveyed the sky in more detail and with greater accuracy. The first great star atlas was produced in 1603 by Johann Bayer, a lawyer in Augsburg with a passion for astronomy. His *Uranometria* atlas devoted one large chart to each of the forty-eight Ptolemaic constellations, using star positions from Ptolemy's catalogue and from the great Danish observer Tycho Brahe, who measured the most accurate star positions in the pre-telescopic era; the southern skies not in Ptolemy's catalogue were allocated one map, depicting the twelve new constellations created by the Dutch navigator Pieter Dirkszoon Keyser. In all, over 2000 stars are plotted, twice as many as shown by Dürer. So popular was the *Uranometria* that it was reissued several times throughout the seventeenth century; its exquisitely engraved charts are true works of art.

Johann Bayer, a German lawyer, produced a landmark star atlas in 1603 called *Uranometria*, in which he devoted individual charts to each of the 48 Greek constellations, plus one plate to the 12 new southern constellations of Keyser and de Houtman. The beautiful plates were engraved by Alexander Mair. Here Hercules is seen holding a branch from the golden apple tree of the Hesperides. Bayer's *Uranometria* was highly popular on account of its comprehensiveness, its artistic quality and that it introduced the system of labelling stars with Greek letters. (Institute of Astronomy Library, University of Cambridge)

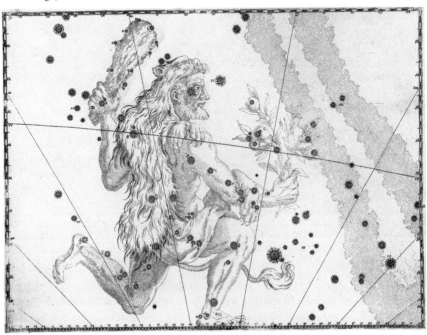

Bayer's atlas was notable for another reason: it introduced the system of labelling bright stars by Greek letters, a system that astronomers still use. For example, the bright star Betelgeuse is also known as Alpha Orionis, meaning Alpha of Orion (the genitive case of the constellation is always used). Since the measurement of star brightnesses was not a very precise art in those days, the sequence of Greek letters assigned by Bayer only approximately follows the sequence of stellar brightnesses in each constellation. In a number of cases, the star marked Alpha is not the brightest – as in the case of Orion, where Beta Orionis (Rigel) is the brightest star. Gemini is another constellation in which the star Beta is brighter than Alpha.

Bayer did not assign Greek letters to the southern constellations of Keyser, perhaps reasoning that such a move would be premature. The Bayer lettering system was extended to the southernmost constellations 160 years later by the French astronomer Nicolas Louis de Lacaille, on his map of the southern skies published in 1763. Constellations of the northern sky that were introduced subsequent to Bayer's time were allocated Greek letters by the English astronomer Francis Baily in the British Association's star catalogue of 1845.

A few years after Bayer's *Uranometria* appeared, astronomy was revolutionized by the invention of the telescope, which not only showed faint stars that had hitherto been invisible but also greatly improved the accuracy by which star positions could be measured. One man remained unmoved by this advance: Johannes Hevelius, an astronomer from Danzig (the modern Gdansk in Poland). Stubbornly, Hevelius continued to measure star positions with naked-eye sights throughout his life, worrying that lenses might introduce positional distortions.

Hevelius's catalogue of over 1500 star positions was published post-humously in 1690; accompanying the catalogue was an atlas called *Firmamentum Sobiescianum* engraved by Hevelius himself. For the southern stars Hevelius used the observations made by the English astronomer Edmond Halley from the island of St Helena, improving on the work of the pioneering Dutchmen Pieter Dirkszoon Keyser and Frederick de Houtman.

Firmamentum Sobiescianum suffers from the drawback that the constellation figures are depicted back to front, as they would appear on a celestial globe; this makes it difficult for an observer to match up the star patterns to the real sky. For this reason the Hevelius maps are not used for the constellation illustrations in this book.

Celestial mapping took another major stride in the eighteenth century with the work of the first Astronomer Royal, John Flamsteed, who catalogued nearly 3000 stars with unprecedented precision from the Royal Observatory at Greenwich. Flamsteed's star catalogue, *Historia Coelestis Britannica*, was published posthumously in 1725, followed four years later by *Atlas Coelestis*, a set of twenty-five maps based entirely on Flamsteed's own observations. The far southern skies, below the horizon of Greenwich, are covered by one small chart that depicts the twelve constellations of Keyser and de Houtman plus Halley's Robur Carolinum.

Johannes Hevelius, a seventeenth-century Polish astronomer, produced an influential star atlas, *Firmamentum Sobiescianum*, published posthumously in 1690. The plates were engraved by Hevelius himself. Hevelius introduced eleven new constellations, of which seven are still accepted by astronomers. His atlas showed the constellation figures from the rear, as they would appear on a celestial globe. On this plate Bootes is shown holding the lead of the hunting dogs, Canes Venatici. (Institute of Astronomy Library, University of Cambridge).

Flamsteed took particular care to depict the constellation figures exactly as Ptolemy had described them. The introduction to *Atlas Coelestis* contains some disapproving words about the way that Bayer had represented the constellation figures in his *Uranometria*:

> Having drawn all his human figures, except Boötes, Andromeda and Virgo, with their backs towards us, those stars, which all before him place in the right shoulders, sides, hands, legs or feet, fall in the left, and the contrary . . . whereby he renders the oldest observations false or nonsense.

Despite popular misconception, Flamsteed did not introduce the so-called Flamsteed number system for identifying the stars in each constellation; that was done in 1783 by the Frenchman J.J. Lalande. In a French edition of Flamsteed's catalogue Lalande added a column in which he numbered the stars consecutively in each constellation in the order that Flamsteed had listed them, and this is the system that astronomers mean when they speak of Flamsteed numbers. Stars are usually referred to by their Flamsteed numbers – for example, 61 Cygni or 70 Ophiuchi – only when they are not already identified by a Greek letter.

Flamsteed's catalogue and atlas set new standards in astronomy, and I have used his atlas as one of the sources for illustrations in this book. The other source is the *Uranographia* star atlas published in 1801 by the German astronomer Johann Elert Bode, director of Berlin Observatory. Bode's *Uranographia* was the first atlas to depict virtually all the stars visible to the naked eye (i.e. down to sixth magnitude), plus a fair selection of stars down to six times fainter (eighth magnitude). Over 17,000 stars are plotted, taken from the observations of various astronomers including Flamsteed, Lacaille, Lalande and Bode himself. Bode intended the *Uranographia* to be comprehensive – and he certainly succeeded, for in addition to charting a greater number of stars than any previous cartographer he also depicted more constellations, over 100 of them.

Bode's *Uranographia*, the greatest of the old-style pictorial star atlases, marked the end of an era. From Bode's time on, astronomers placed decreasing emphasis on the fanciful (and physically meaningless) constellation figures of the Greeks, concentrating instead on the exact measurement of position, brightness and physical properties of the stars.

By the end of the nineteenth century, 2000 years of Greek tradition had finally given way to the facts-and-figures approach of astronomical census-takers and statisticians. Where the ancient Greeks imagined their gods and heroes populating the sky, modern astronomers have discovered the existence of an equally fantastic pantheon of objects with names such as red giants, white dwarfs, Cepheid variables, pulsars, quasars and black holes.

CHAPTER THREE

—*The celestial eighty-eight*—

— *Andromeda* —

PERHAPS THE MOST ENDURING OF GREEK MYTHS IS THE STORY OF PERSEUS AND ANDROMEDA, THE ORIGINAL VERSION OF GEORGE and the dragon. Its heroine is beautiful Andromeda, the daughter of the weak King Cepheus of Ethiopia and the vain Queen Cassiopeia, whose boastfulness knew no bounds.

Andromeda's misfortunes began one day when her mother claimed that she was more beautiful even than the Nereids, a particularly alluring group of sea nymphs. The affronted Nereids decided that Cassiopeia's vanity had finally gone too far and they asked Poseidon, the sea god, to teach her a lesson. In retribution, Poseidon sent a terrible monster (some say also a flood) to ravage the coast of King Cepheus's territory. Dismayed at the destruction, and with his subjects clamouring for action, the beleaguered Cepheus appealed to the Oracle of Ammon for a solution. He was told that he must sacrifice his virgin daughter to appease the monster.

Hence the blameless Andromeda came to be chained to a rock to atone for the sins of her mother, who watched from the shore with bitter remorse. The site of this event is said to have been on the Mediterranean coast at Joppa (Jaffa), the modern Tel-Aviv. As Andromeda stood on the wave-lashed cliffs, pale with terror and weeping pitifully at her impending fate, the hero Perseus happened by, fresh from his exploit of beheading Medusa the Gorgon. His heart was captivated by the sight of the frail beauty in distress below.

The Roman poet Ovid tells us in his book the *Metamorphoses* that Perseus at first almost mistook her for a marble statue. Only the wind ruffling her hair and the warm tears on her cheeks showed that she was human. Perseus asked her name and why she was chained there. Shy Andromeda, totally different in character from her vainglorious mother, did not at first reply; even though awaiting a horrible death in the monster's slavering jaws, she would have hidden her face modestly in her hands, had they not been bound to the rock.

Perseus persisted in his questioning. Eventually, afraid that her silence

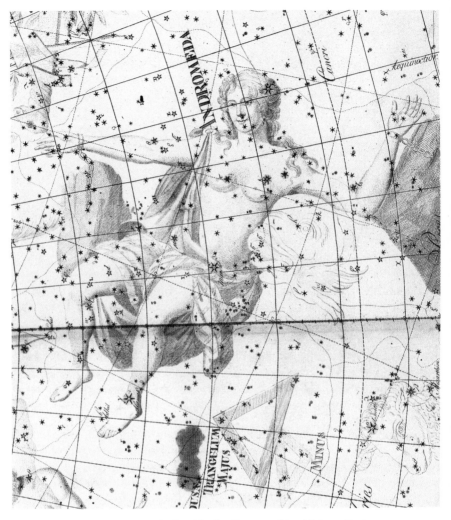

Andromeda chained to a rock, depicted in the *Uranographia* of Johann Bode.

might be misinterpreted as guilt, she told Perseus her story, but broke off with a scream as she saw the monster breasting through the waves towards her. Pausing politely to ask the permission of her parents for Andromeda's hand in marriage, Perseus swooped down, killed the monster with his sword, released the swooning Andromeda to the applause of the onlookers and claimed her for his bride. Andromeda later bore Perseus six children including Perses, ancestor of the Persians, and Gorgophonte, father of Tyndareus, king of Sparta.

It is said that the Greek goddess Athene placed Andromeda's image among the stars, where she lies between Perseus and her mother Cassiopeia. Only the constellation of Pisces, the Fishes, separates her from the Sea Monster, Cetus. Star maps picture Andromeda with her hands in chains.

Her head is marked by the second-magnitude star Alpha Andromedae, originally shared by Andromeda and Pegasus, where it marked the horse's navel. It is known by the two alternative names of Alpheratz or Sirrah. These names come from the Arabic *al-faras*, meaning 'the horse', and *surrat*, meaning 'navel'. The star is now assigned exclusively to Andromeda.

Her waist is marked by the star Beta Andromedae, also called Mirach, a name corrupted from the Arabic *al-mi'zar* meaning 'the girdle' or 'loin cloth'. Her foot is marked by Gamma Andromedae, whose name is variously spelled Almach or Alamak, from the Arabic *al-'anaq*, referring to the desert lynx or caracal which the old Arabs visualized here. Through small telescopes this is a beautiful twin star of contrasting yellow and blue colours.

The most celebrated object in the constellation is the great spiral galaxy M31, positioned on Andromeda's right hip, where it is visible as an elongated blur to the naked eye on clear nights. M31 is a whirlpool of stars similar to our own Milky Way. At a distance of two million light years, the Andromeda galaxy is the farthest object visible to the naked eye.

Antlia
— *the air pump* —

One of the constellations of the southern sky introduced by Nicolas Louis de Lacaille in 1756. He called it Antlia Pneumatica on his map of 1763, and showed it as the type of pump invented by the French physicist Denis Papin. Not surprisingly, there are no legends associated with this constellation and it contains no bright stars or other objects of note.

The air pump shown in the *Uranographia* of Johann Bode under the name Antlia Pneumatica.

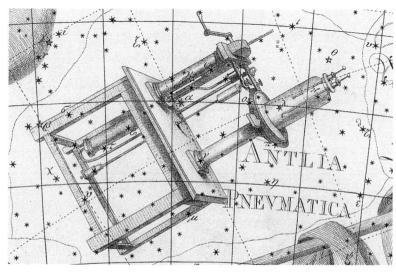

Apus
— *the bird of paradise* —

One of the southern constellations introduced by the Dutch navigators Pieter Dirkszoon Keyser and Frederick de Houtman at the end of the sixteenth century. Apus represents a fabulous bird of paradise, as found in New Guinea. The constellation was depicted on the 1603 star map of Johann Bayer under the name of Apis Indica. It has no named stars, nor are there any legends associated with it.

Apus seen in the *Uranographia* of Johann Bode, where it was given the alternative title Avis Indica, the Indian bird.

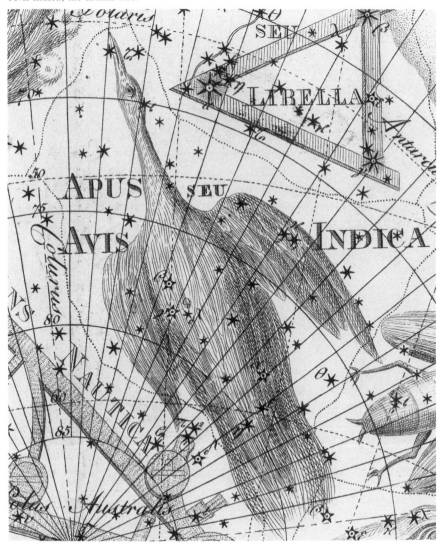

Aquarius
— *the water carrier* —

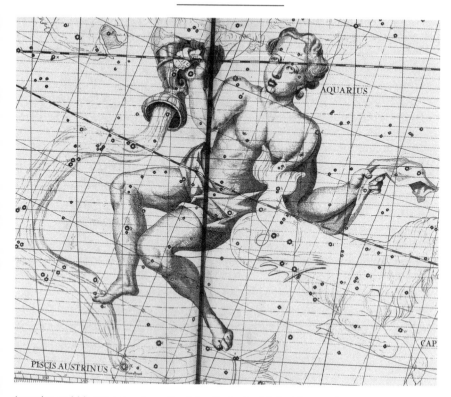

Aquarius and his water jar, from the *Atlas Coelestis* of John Flamsteed.

Star maps show Aquarius as a young man pouring water from a jar, though Ovid, in his *Fasti*, says it is a mixture of water and nectar, the drink of the gods. The stream ends in the mouth of the Southern Fish, Piscis Austrinus. But who is Aquarius? The most popular identification is that he is Ganymede or Ganymedes, said to have been the most beautiful boy alive. He was the son of King Tros, who gave Troy its name. One day, while Ganymede was watching over his father's sheep, Zeus became infatuated with the shepherd boy and swooped down on the Trojan plain in the form of an eagle, carrying Ganymede up to Olympus (or, according to another version, sent an eagle to do it for him). The eagle is commemorated in the neighbouring constellation of Aquila.

In another version of the myth, Ganymede was first carried off by Eos, goddess of the dawn, who had a passion for young men, and Zeus then stole Ganymede from her. Ganymede became wine-waiter to the gods, dispensing nectar from his bowl, to the annoyance of Zeus's wife Hera. Robert Graves tells us that this myth became highly popular in ancient Greece and Rome where it was regarded as signifying divine endorsement for homosexuality. The Latin translation of the name Ganymede gave rise to the word catamite.

If this myth seems insubstantial to us, it is perhaps a result of the Greeks imposing their own story on a constellation adopted from elsewhere. The constellation of the water pourer originally seems to have represented the Egyptian god of the Nile – but, as Robert Graves says, the Greeks were not much interested in the Nile.

Germanicus Caesar identifies the constellation with Deucalion, son of Prometheus, one of the few men to escape the great flood. 'Deucalion pours forth water, that hostile element he once fled, and in so doing draws attention to his small pitcher', wrote Germanicus. Hyginus offers the additional identification of the constellation with Cecrops, an early king of Athens, seen making sacrifices to the gods using water, for he ruled in the days before wine was made.

Several stars in Aquarius have names beginning with 'Sad'. In Arabic, *sa'd* means 'luck'. Alpha Aquarii is called Sadalmelik, from *sa'd al-malik*, usually translated as 'the lucky stars of the king'. Beta Aquarii is called Sadalsuud, from *sa'd al-su'ud*, possibly meaning 'luckiest of the lucky'. Gamma Aquarii is Sadachbia, from *sa'd al-akhbiya*, possibly meaning 'lucky stars of the tents'. The exact significance of these names has been lost even by the Arabs, according to the German expert on star names, Paul Kunitzsch.

Aquila
— *the eagle* —

Aquila represents an eagle, the thunderbird of the Greeks. There are several explanations for this eagle in the sky. In Greek and Roman mythology, the eagle was the bird of Zeus, carrying (and returning) the thunderbolts which the wrathful god hurled at his enemies. But the eagle was involved in love as well as war.

According to one story, Aquila is the eagle that snatched up the beautiful Trojan boy Ganymede, son of King Tros, to become the cup-bearer of the gods. Authorities such as the Roman poet Ovid say that Zeus turned himself into an eagle, whereas others say that the eagle was simply sent by Zeus. Ganymede himself is represented by the neighbouring constellation of Aquarius, and star charts show Aquila swooping down towards Aquarius. Germanicus Caesar says that the eagle is guarding the arrow of Eros (neighbouring Sagitta) which made Zeus love-struck.

The constellations of the eagle and the swan are linked in an account by Hyginus. Zeus fell in love with the goddess Nemesis but, when she resisted his advances, he turned himself into a swan and had Aphrodite pretend to

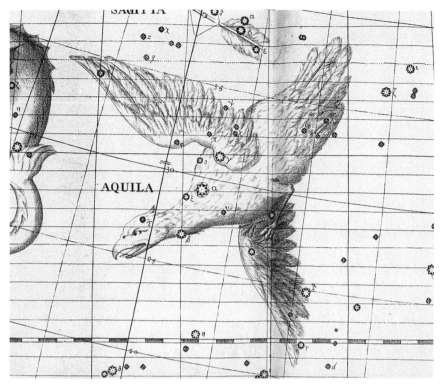

Aquila swooping across Flamsteed's *Atlas Coelestis*. Its brightest star, Altair, lies in its neck and is labelled Alpha.

pursue him in the form of an eagle. Nemesis gave refuge to the escaping swan, only to find herself in the embrace of Zeus. To commemorate this successful trick, Zeus placed the images of swan and eagle in the sky.

The name of the constellation's brightest star, Altair, comes from the Arabic *al-nasr al-ta'ir*, meaning 'flying eagle' or 'vulture'. Ptolemy called it Aetus, the eagle, the same name as the constellation. The German scholar Paul Kunitzsch notes that the Babylonians and Sumerians referred to Altair as the eagle star. Altair's neighbouring stars Beta and Gamma Aquilae form the eagle's outstretched wings. These two stars have their own names, Alshain and Tarazed, which come from a Persian translation of an old Arabic word meaning 'the balance'.

Altair forms one corner of the so-called Summer Triangle with the stars Vega and Deneb, found in the constellations Lyra and Cygnus respectively. A charming eastern myth visualizes the stars of Aquila and the stars of Lyra as two lovers separated by the river of the Milky Way, able to meet on just one day each year when magpies collect to form a bridge across the celestial river.

The southern part of Aquila was subdivided by Ptolemy into a now-obsolete constellation called Antinous, visualized on some maps as being held in the eagle's claws (see Chapter Four).

Ara
— *the altar* —

Altars feature frequently in Greek legend, for heroes were always making sacrifices to the gods, so it is not surprising to find an altar among the stars. But this altar is a special one, for it was used by the gods themselves to swear a vow of allegiance before their fight against the Titans, according to Eratosthenes and Manilius. That clash was one of the most significant events in Greek myth.

At that time the ruler of the Universe was Cronus, one of the twelve Titans. Cronus had overthrown his father, Uranus, but it was prophesied that he would be deposed by one of his own sons. In a desperate attempt to forestall the prophesy, Cronus swallowed his children as they were born: Hestia, Demeter, Hera, Hades and Poseidon, all ultimately destined to become gods and goddesses. At last, his wife, Rhea, could not bear to see any more children swallowed. She smuggled the next child, Zeus, to the cave of Dicte in Crete and gave Cronus a stone to swallow instead, telling him it was the infant Zeus.

On Crete, Zeus grew up safely. When he reached maturity he returned to his father's palace and forced Cronus to vomit up the children he had swallowed, who emerged as fully grown gods and goddesses. Zeus and his

Ara, the altar, depicted with its smoke rising southwards in the *Uranographia* of Johann Bode.

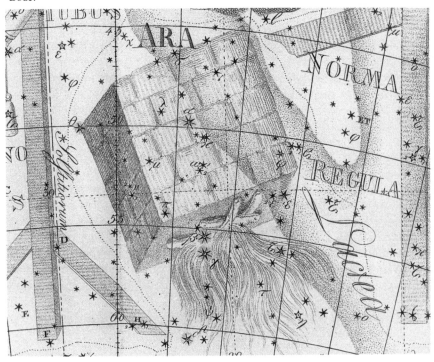

brother gods then set up an altar and vowed on it to overthrow the callous rule of Cronus and the other Titans.

The battle raged ten years between the Titans, led by Atlas, on Mount Othrys and the gods led by Zeus on Mount Olympus. To break the deadlock, Mother Earth (Gaia) instructed Zeus to release the ugly brothers of the Titans, whom Cronus had imprisoned in the sunless caves of Tartarus, the lowermost region of the Underworld. There were two sets of brothers, the Hecatoncheires (hundred-handed giants) and the one-eyed Cyclopes, and they wanted revenge against Cronus. Zeus stole down to Tartarus, released the monstrous creatures and asked them to join him in the battle raging above. Delighted by their unexpected freedom, the Cyclopes set to work to help the gods. They fashioned a helmet of darkness for Hades, a trident for Poseidon and, above all, thunderbolts for Zeus. With these new weapons and their monstrous allies the gods routed the Titans.

After their victory, the gods cast lots to divide up the Universe. Poseidon became lord of the sea, Hades won the underworld and Zeus was allotted the sky. Zeus then placed the altar of the gods in the sky as the constellation Ara in lasting gratitude for their victory over the Titans.

The Greeks regarded Ara as a sign of storms at sea. According to Aratus, if the altar was visible while other stars were covered by cloud, mariners could expect southerly gales.

Originally the Greeks visualized the altar with its smoke rising north-wards, but since the atlas of Johann Bayer in 1603 it has been depicted with its top facing southwards. Atlases also show Ara as the altar on which Centaurus is about to sacrifice Lupus, the Wolf.

Aries
— *the ram* —

It is not surprising to find a ram in the sky, for rams were frequently sacrificed to the gods, and Zeus was at times identified with a ram. But the mythographers agree that Aries is a special ram, the one whose golden fleece was the object of the voyage of Jason and the Argonauts. The ram made its appearance on Earth just as King Athamas of Boeotia was about to sacrifice his son Phrixus to ward off an impending famine.

King Athamas and his wife Nephele had an unhappy marriage, so Athamas turned instead to Ino, daughter of King Cadmus from neighbour-ing Thebes. Ino resented her step-children, Phrixus and Helle, and she arranged a plot to have them killed. She began by parching the wheat so that the crops would fail. When Athamas appealed for help to the Delphic Oracle, Ino bribed messengers to bring back a false reply that Phrixus must be sacrificed to save the harvest.

Reluctantly, Athamas took his son to the top of Mount Laphystium,

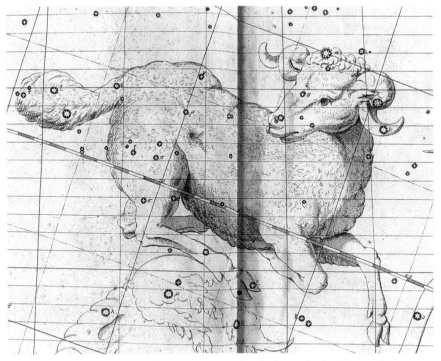

Aries, the ram with the golden fleece, from the *Atlas Coelestis* of John Flamsteed.

overlooking his palace at Orchomenus. He was about to sacrifice Phrixus to Zeus when Nephele intervened to save her son, sending down from the sky a winged ram with a golden fleece. Phrixus climbed on the ram's back and was joined by his sister Helle, who feared for her own life. They flew off eastwards to Colchis, which lay on the eastern shore of the Black Sea, under the Caucasus Mountains (the modern Soviet Georgia). On the way Helle's grip failed, and she fell into the channel between Europe and Asia, the Dardanelles, which the Greeks named the Hellespont in her memory. On reaching Colchis, Phrixus sacrificed the ram in gratitude to Zeus. He presented its golden fleece to the fearsome King Aeetes of Colchis who, in return, gave Phrixus the hand of his daughter Chalciope.

After Phrixus died his ghost returned to Greece to haunt his cousin Pelias, who had seized the throne of Iolcus in Thessaly. The true successor to the throne was Jason. Pelias promised to give up the throne to Jason if he brought home the golden fleece from Colchis. This was the challenge that led to the epic voyage of Jason and the Argonauts.

When he reached Colchis, Jason first asked King Aeetes politely for the fleece, which hung on an oak in a sacred wood, guarded by a huge unsleeping serpent. King Aeetes rejected Jason's request. Fortunately for the expedition, the king's daughter, Medea, fell in love with Jason and offered to help him steal the fleece. At night the two crept into the wood where the golden fleece hung, shining like a cloud lit by the rising Sun.

Medea bewitched the serpent so that it slept while Jason snatched the fleece. According to Apollonius Rhodius, the fleece was as large as the hide of a young cow, and when Jason slung it over his shoulder it reached his feet. The ground shone from its glittering golden wool as Jason and Medea escaped with it. Once free of the pursuing forces of King Aeetes, Jason and Medea used the fleece to cover their wedding bed. The final resting place of the fleece was in the temple of Zeus at Orchomenus, where Jason hung it on his return to Greece.

On old star maps the ram is shown in a crouching position, but without wings, its head turned towards Taurus. In the sky it is not at all prominent. Its most noticeable feature is a bent line of three stars, which mark its head. Of these three stars, Alpha Arietis is called Hamal, from the Arabic for lamb; Beta Arietis is Sheratan, from the Arabic meaning 'two' of something (possibly two signs or two horns, for it was originally applied both to this star and to its neighbour, Gamma Arietis); and Gamma Arietis is Mesarthim, a curiously corrupted form of *al-sharatan*, the title which it originally shared with Beta Arietis.

In astronomy, Aries assumes a far greater importance than its brightness would suggest, for in Greek times it contained the cardinal point known as the vernal equinox. This is the point at which the Sun crosses the celestial equator from north to south. But the vernal equinox is not stationary, because of the slow wobble of the Earth's axis known as precession.

When the great Greek astronomer Hipparchus defined the position of the vernal equinox around 130 BC this point lay south of the star Mesarthim (Gamma Arietis). The zodiac was then taken to start from here, and so the vernal equinox was commonly known as the first point of Aries. Because of precession, the vernal equinox has moved some 30 degrees since the time of Hipparchus and currently lies in the neighbouring constellation Pisces. Despite this, the vernal equinox is still sometimes called the first point of Aries.

Auriga
— *the charioteer* —

This prominent constellation has several identifications in mythology. The most popular interpretation is that he is Erichthonius, a legendary king of Athens. He was the son of Hephaestus the god of fire, better known by his Roman name of Vulcan, but he was raised by the goddess Athene, after whom Athens is named. In her honour Erichthonius instituted a festival called the Panathenaea.

Athene taught Erichthonius many skills, including how to tame horses. He became the first person to harness four horses to a chariot, in imitation of the four-horse chariot of the Sun, a bold move which gained him the admiration of Zeus and assured him a place among the stars. There,

Auriga carrying the goat and kids, from the *Uranographia* of Johann Bode. The bright star Capella lies in the body of the goat.

Erichthonius is depicted at the reins, perhaps participating in the Panathenaic games in which he frequently drove his chariot to victory.

Another identification is that Auriga is really Myrtilus, the charioteer of King Oenomaus of Elis and son of Hermes. The king had a beautiful daughter, Hippodamia, whom he was determined not to let go. He challenged each of her suitors to a death-or-glory chariot race. They were to speed away with Hippodamia on their chariots, but if Oenomaus caught up with them before they reached Corinth he would kill them. Since he had the swiftest chariot in Greece, skilfully driven by Myrtilus, no man had yet survived the test.

A dozen suitors had been beheaded by the time that Pelops, the handsome son of Tantalus, came to claim Hippodamia's hand. Hippodamia, falling in love with him on sight, begged Myrtilus to betray the king so that Pelops might win the race. Myrtilus, who was himself secretly in love with Hippodamia, tampered with the pins holding the wheels on Oenomaus' chariot. During the pursuit of Pelops, the wheels of the king's chariot fell off and Oenomaus was thrown to his death.

Hippodamia was now left in the company of both Pelops and Myrtilus. Pelops solved the awkward situation by unceremoniously throwing Myrtilus into the sea, from where he cursed the house of Pelops as he drowned. Hermes put the image of his son Myrtilus into the sky as the constellation Auriga. Germanicus Caesar supports this identification because, he says, 'you will observe that he has no chariot, and, his reins broken, is sorrowful, grieving that Hippodamia has been taken away by the treachery of Pelops'.

A third identification of Auriga is Hippolytus, son of Theseus, whose stepmother Phaedra fell in love with him. When Hippolytus rejected her, she hanged herself in despair. Theseus banished Hippolytus from Athens. As he drove away his chariot was wrecked, killing him. Asclepius the healer brought the blameless Hippolytus back to life again, a deed for which Zeus struck Asclepius down with a thunderbolt at the demand of Hades, who was annoyed at losing a valuable soul.

Auriga contains the sixth-brightest star in the sky, Capella, a Roman name meaning 'she-goat' (its Greek name was Aix). Ptolemy described this star as being on the charioteer's left shoulder. According to Aratus it represented the goat Amaltheia, who suckled the infant Zeus on the island of Crete and was placed in the sky as a mark of gratitude, along with the two kids she bore at the same time. The kids, frequently known by their Latin name of Haedi (Eriphi in Greek), are represented by the neighbouring stars Eta and Zeta Aurigae.

An alternative story is that Amaltheia was the nymph who owned the goat. Eratosthenes says that the goat was so ugly that it terrified the Titans who ruled the Earth at that time. When Zeus grew up and challenged the Titans for supremacy, he made a cloak from the goat's hide, the back of which looked like the head of the Gorgon. This horrible-looking goatskin formed the so-called aegis of Zeus (the word aegis actually means 'goatskin'). The aegis protected Zeus and scared his enemies, a particular advantage in his fight against the Titans.

Some early writers spoke of the Goat and Kids as a separate constellation, but since the time of Ptolemy they have been awkwardly combined with the Charioteer, the goat resting on the charioteer's shoulder, with the kids supported on his wrist. There is no legend to explain why the charioteer is so encumbered with livestock.

Greek astronomers regarded one star as being shared by Auriga and Taurus, representing the right foot of the charioteer and the tip of the bull's left horn, as old star maps show it. Modern astronomers now assign this star exclusively to Taurus.

Boötes
— *the herdsman* —

This constellation (pronounced Boh-oh-tease) is closely linked in legend with the Great Bear, Ursa Major, because of its position behind the bear's tail. The origin of the name Boötes is not certain, but it probably comes from a Greek word meaning 'noisy' or 'clamorous', referring to the herdsman's shouts to his animals. An alternative explanation is that the name comes from the ancient Greek meaning 'ox-driver', from the fact that

Boötes shown standing on Mons Maenalus, an obsolete sub-constellation. Above his head the obsolete constellation, Quadrans Muralis. From *Uranographia* by Johann Bode.

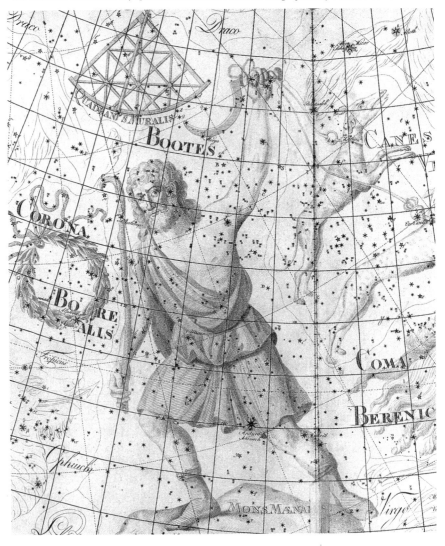

Ursa Major was sometimes visualized as a cart pulled by oxen. The Greeks also knew this constellation as Arctophylax, variously translated as Bear Watcher, Bear Keeper or Bear Guard.

According to a story that goes back to Eratosthenes, the constellation represents Arcas, son of the god Zeus and Callisto, daughter of King Lycaon of Arcadia. One day Zeus came to dine with his father-in-law Lycaon, an unusual thing for a god to do. To test whether his guest really was the great Zeus, Lycaon cut up Arcas and served him as part of a mixed grill (some say that this deed was done not by Lycaon but by his sons). Zeus easily recognized the flesh of his son. In a burning rage, he tipped over the table, scattering the feast, killed the sons of Lycaon with a thunderbolt, and turned Lycaon into a wolf. Then Zeus collected the parts of Arcas, made them whole again and gave his son to Maia the Pleiad to bring up.

Meanwhile, Callisto had been turned into a bear, some say by Zeus's wife Hera out of jealousy, or by Zeus himself to disguise his paramour from Hera's revenge, or even by Artemis to punish Callisto for losing her virginity. Whatever the case, when Arcas had grown into a strapping teenager he came across this bear while hunting in the woods. Callisto recognized her son, but though she tried to greet him warmly she could only growl. Not surprisingly, Arcas failed to interpret this expression of motherly love and began to chase the bear. With Arcas in hot pursuit, Callisto fled into the temple of Zeus, a forbidden place where trespassers were punished by death. Zeus snatched up Arcas and his mother and placed them in the sky as the constellations of the bear and the bear keeper. The Greek poet Aratus visualized Boötes as a man driving the bear around the pole. Later astronomers have given Boötes two dogs, in the form of the neighbouring constellation Canes Venatici.

A second legend identifies Boötes with Icarius (not to be confused with Icarus, son of Daedalus). According to this tale, recounted at length by Hyginus in *Poetic Astronomy* (II.4), the god Dionysus taught Icarius how to cultivate vines and make wine. When he offered some of his new vintage to shepherds, they became so intoxicated that their friends thought they had been poisoned, and in revenge they killed Icarius.

His dog Maera fled home howling and led Icarius's daughter Erigone to where his body lay beneath a tree. In despair, Erigone hanged herself from the tree; even the dog died, either of grief or by drowning itself. Zeus put Icarius into the sky as Boötes, his daughter Erigone became the constellation Virgo and the dog became Canis Minor or Canis Major (according to different authorities).

Boötes contains the fourth-brightest star in the entire sky, Arcturus, mentioned by Homer, Hesiod and Ptolemy. Its name means 'bear guard' in Greek. Germanicus Caesar said that Arcturus 'lies where his garment is fastened by a knot', but Ptolemy placed it between the thighs, which is where mapmakers have depicted it. Astronomers have found that Arcturus is a red giant star about twenty-four times larger than the Sun, lying thirty-six light years away.

Caelum
— the chisel —

This small and insignificant constellation in the southern hemisphere is one of the inventions of the eighteenth-century French astronomer Nicolas Louis de Lacaille. He introduced it on his map of the southern stars in 1756 under the French name les Burins. On a map of 1763 this was Latinized to Caelum Scalptorium, since shortened. It was depicted as a pair of crossed burins (sharp engraving tools). There are no legends associated with the constellation and its stars are faint.

Caelum shown as Caela Scalptoris in the *Uranographia* of Johann Bode.

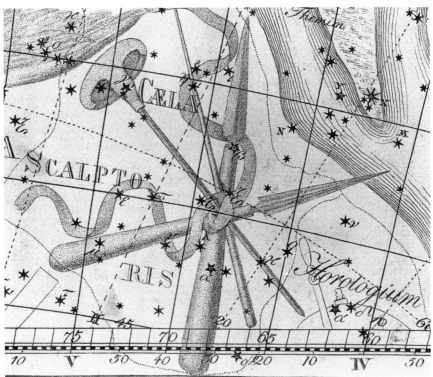

Camelopardalis
— the giraffe —

One of the most unlikely animals to be found in the sky is a giraffe. The constellation Camelopardalis was invented in 1613 by the Dutch theologian and astronomer Petrus Plancius. It lies in an area between the head of the Great Bear and Cassiopeia, a region that was left blank by the Greeks since it contains no stars brighter than fourth magnitude. The constellation supposedly represents the animal on which Rebecca rode into Canaan for her marriage to Isaac. The German astronomer Jacob Bartsch showed the constellation on his map of 1624 and wrongly attributed its invention to Isaac Habrecht of Strasbourg, who had shown the constellation on his star globe of 1621. The constellation's name is sometimes wrongly spelled Camelopardalus.

The top part of the large constellation Camelopardalis, shown in the *Uranographia* of Johann Bode. Above it lie two obsolete constellations: Rangifer, the reindeer, and Custos Messium, the harvest keeper (see Chapter Four).

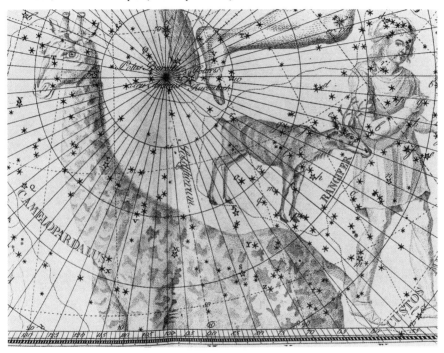

Cancer
— *the crab* —

The crab is a minor character in one of the labours of Heracles (the Greek name for Hercules). While Heracles was fighting the multi-headed monster called the Hydra in the swamp near Lerna, the crab emerged from the swamp and added its own attack by biting Heracles on the foot. Heracles angrily stamped on the crab, crushing it. For this modest contribution to history, we are told that the goddess Hera, the enemy of Heracles, put the crab among the stars of the zodiac. Fittingly enough for such a minor character, it is the faintest of the zodiacal constellations, with no star brighter than fourth magnitude. The star Alpha Cancri is named Acubens, from the Arabic meaning 'claw'.

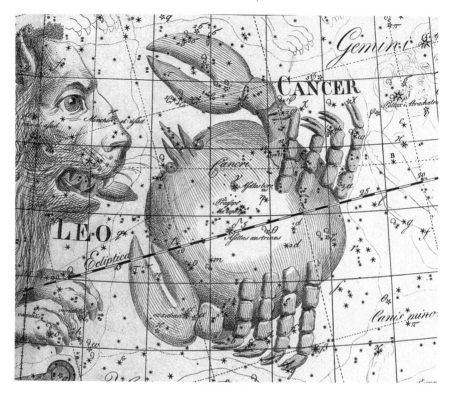

Cancer, from the *Uranographia* of Johann Bode. At its centre lies the star cluster Praesepe, flanked by the stars Asellus Borealis and Asellus Australis

Two stars in the constellation are named Asellus Borealis and Asellus Australis, Latin names meaning the 'northern ass' and 'southern ass', and they have their own legend. According to Eratosthenes, during the battle between the gods and the Giants that followed the overthrow of the Titans, the gods Dionysus, Hephaestus and some companions came riding on donkeys to join in the fray. The Giants had never heard the braying of donkeys before, and they took flight at the noise, thinking that some dreadful monster was about to be unleashed upon them. Dionysus put the asses in the sky, either side of a cluster of stars which the Greeks called Phatne, the Manger, from which the asses seem to be feeding. Ptolemy described Phatne as 'the nebulous mass in the chest'. Astronomers now know this star cluster by its Latin name Praesepe, but it is popularly termed the Beehive (*praesepe* can mean both 'manger' and 'hive').

The tropic of Cancer is the latitude on Earth at which the Sun appears overhead at noon on the summer solstice, June 21. In the time of the ancient Greeks the Sun lay among the stars of Cancer on this date, but the wobble of the Earth on its axis, called precession, has moved the summer solstice to a point on the borders of Gemini and Taurus.

Canes Venatici
— *the hunting dogs* —

The Polish astronomer Johannes Hevelius formed this constellation in 1687 from stars that had previously been considered part of Ursa Major. Canes Venatici represents two dogs held on a lead by Boötes, snapping at the heels of the Great Bear. The southern dog is represented by the two brightest stars in the constellation, Alpha and Beta Canum Venaticorum.

The star Alpha is known as Cor Caroli, meaning Charles's Heart, in honour of King Charles I of England. It was given this title by Sir Charles Scarborough, physician to King Charles II. Scarborough said that the star shone particularly brightly on the night of 29 May 1660, when King Charles II returned to London at the Restoration of the Monarchy. There has been much confusion over which King Charles the star is supposed to commemorate because of this, but it definitely refers to the first King Charles. It was originally shown in 1673 on a star map by the English cartographer Francis Lamb under the name Cor Caroli Regis Martyris, a reference to the fact that King Charles I was beheaded. Lamb and others, such as the Englishman

Canes Venatici, two hunting dogs held on a leash by Bootes, from the *Atlas Coelestis* of John Flamsteed.

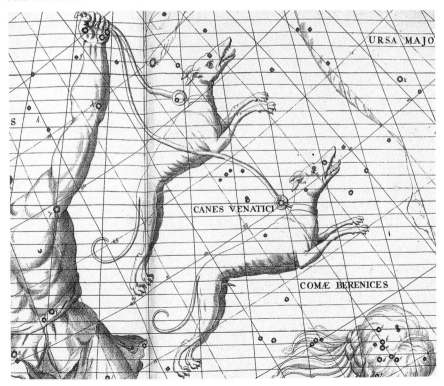

Edward Sherburne in 1675, drew a heart around the star surmounted by a crown, turning it into a mini-constellation.

The star Beta is called Chara, from the Greek for 'joy', the name given by Hevelius to the southern dog. The northern dog, called Asterion (starry), is marked only by a scattering of faint stars. Bode drew the dogs wih their names written on their collars.

Canes Venatici contains a globular cluster of stars, M3, and a beautiful spiral galaxy, M51, called the Whirlpool. M51 was the first galaxy in which spiral form was noticed, by the Irish astronomer Lord Rosse in 1845. It consists of a large galaxy in near-collision with a smaller one.

Canis major
— *the great dog* —

Canis Major is dominated by the star Sirius, popularly called the Dog Star, the most brilliant star in the entire sky; almost certainly the constellation originated with this star alone. Aratus referred to Canis Major as the guard-dog of Orion, following on the heels of its master, and standing on its hind legs with Sirius carried in its jaws. Manilius called it 'the dog with the blazing face'. Canis Major seems to cross the sky in pursuit of the hare, represented by the constellation Lepus under Orion's feet.

Mythologists such as Eratosthenes and Hyginus said that the constellation represented Laelaps, a dog so swift that no prey could escape it. This dog had a long list of owners, one of them being Procris, daughter of King Erechtheus of Athens and wife of Cephalus, but accounts differ about how she came by it. In one version the dog was given to her by Artemis, goddess of hunting; but a more likely account says that it is the dog given by Zeus to Europa, whose son Minos, King of Crete, passed it on to Procris. The dog was presented to her along with a javelin that could never miss; this turned out to be an unlucky gift, for her husband Cephalus accidentally killed her with it while out hunting.

Cephalus inherited the dog, and took it with him to Thebes (not Thebes in Egypt but a town in Boeotia, north of Athens) where a vicious fox was ravaging the countryside. The fox was so swift of foot that it was destined never to be caught – yet Laelaps the hound was destined to catch whatever it pursued. Off they went, almost faster than the eye could follow, the inescapable dog in pursuit of the uncatchable fox. At one moment the dog would seem to have its prey within grasp, but could only close its jaws on thin air as the fox raced ahead of it again. There could be no resolution of such a paradox, so Zeus turned them both to stone, and the dog he placed in the sky as Canis Major, without the fox.

The name of the star Sirius comes from the Greek word *seirius* meaning 'searing' or 'scorching', highly appropriate for something so brilliant. In Greek times its rising at dawn just before the Sun marked the start of the hottest part of the summer, a time that hence became known as the Dog

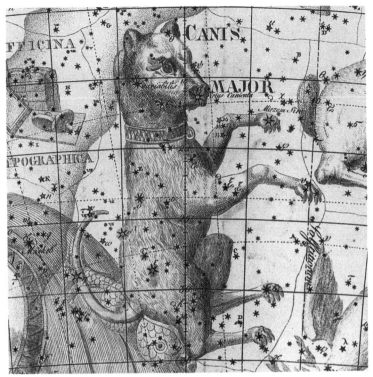

Canis Major, with Sirius marking its snout, shown in the *Uranographia* of Johann Bode.

Days. 'It barks forth flame and doubles the burning heat of the Sun', said Manilius, expressing a belief held by the Greeks and Romans that the star had a heating effect. The ancient Greek writer Hesiod wrote of 'heads and limbs drained dry by Sirius', and Virgil in the *Georgics* said that 'the torrid Dog Star cracks the fields'.

Germanicus Caesar outlined clearly the effects that the rising of Sirius with the Sun was supposed to have. Healthy crops it strengthens, but those with shrivelled leaves or feeble roots it kills. 'There is no star the farmer likes more or hates more', according to Germanicus.

'Hardly is it inferior to the Sun, save that its abode is far away', wrote Manilius, anticipating the modern view that stars are bodies like the Sun only vastly more distant. Yet, in contradiction of the supposed heating effects of Sirius, Manilius continued: 'The beams it launches from its sky-blue face are cold.' That description of the colour of Sirius is in contrast to Ptolemy's surprising reference to it as reddish, which has caused all manner of arguments.

In fact, Manilius was nearly correct, for Sirius is a blue-white star, even larger and brighter than the Sun. It lies 8.7 light years away, making it one of the Sun's closest neighbours. It has a white dwarf companion star, visible only in telescopes, that orbits it every fifty years.

Canis minor
— the little dog —

This constellation originally consisted of just its brightest star Procyon, whose name in Greek means 'before the dog' from the fact that it rises earlier than the other celestial dog, Canis Major. It is a small constellation and contains little of interest other than Procyon itself, a white star 11.3 light years away, the eighth-brightest star in the heavens.

Canis Minor is usually identified as one of the dogs of Orion. But in a famous legend from Attica (the area around Athens), recounted by the mythographer Hyginus, the constellation represents Maera, dog of Icarius, the man whom the god Dionysus first taught to make wine. When Icarius gave his wine to some shepherds for tasting, they rapidly became drunk. Suspecting that Icarius had poisoned them, they killed him. Maera the dog ran howling to Icarius's daughter Erigone, caught hold of her dress by his teeth and led her to her father's body. Both Erigone and the dog took their own lives where Icarius lay. Zeus placed their images among the stars as a reminder of the unfortunate affair. To atone for their tragic mistake, the people of Athens instituted a yearly celebration in honour of Icarius and Erigone. In this story, Icarius is identified with the constellation Boötes, Erigone is Virgo and Maera is Canis Minor.

Canis Minor from the *Uranographia* of Johann Bode. In its body lies the bright star Procyon.

According to Hyginus, the murderers of Icarius fled to the island of Ceos off the coast of Attica, but their wrongdoing followed them. The island was plagued with famine and sickness, attributed in the legend to the scorching effect of the Dog Star (here, Procyon seems to become confused with the greater dog star, Sirius in Canis Major). King Aristaeus of Ceos, son of the god Apollo, asked his father for advice and was told to pray to Zeus for relief. Zeus sent the Etesian winds, which every year blow for forty days from the rising of the Dog Star to cool all of Greece and its islands in the summer heat. After this, the priests of Ceos instituted the practice of making yearly sacrifices before the rising of the Dog Star.

Procyon is of particular interest to astronomers because it has a small, hot companion star called a white dwarf that orbits it every forty years. Coincidentally the other dog star, Sirius, also has one of these small, highly dense white dwarfs as a companion.

Capricornus
— *the sea goat* —

Capricornus is an unlikely looking creature, with the head and forelegs of a goat and the tail of a fish. The constellation evidently originated with the Sumerians and Babylonians, who had a fondness for amphibious creatures; the ancient Sumerians called it SUHUR-MASH-HA, the goat-fish. But to the Greeks, who named it Aegoceros (goat-horned), the constellation was identified with Pan, god of the countryside who had the horns and legs of a goat.

Pan, a playful creature of uncertain parentage, spent much of his time chasing females or sleeping it off with a siesta. He could frighten people with his loud shout, which is the origin of the word 'panic'. One of his offspring was Crotus, identified with the constellation Sagittarius. Pan's attempted seduction of the nymph Syrinx failed when she turned herself into a handful of reeds. As he clutched the reeds the wind blew through them, creating an enchanting sound. Pan selected reeds of different lengths and stuck them together with wax to form the famous pipes of Pan, also called the *syrinx*.

Pan came to the rescue of the gods on two separate occasions. During the battle of the gods and the Titans, Pan blew a conch shell to help put the enemy to flight. According to Eratosthenes his connection with the conch shell accounts for his fishy nature in the sky, although Hyginus says somewhat absurdly that it is because he hurled shellfish at the enemy. On a later occasion Pan shouted a warning to the gods that the monster Typhon was approaching, sent by Mother Earth (Gaea) against the gods. At Pan's suggestion the gods disguised themselves as animals to elude the monster. Pan himself took refuge in a river, turning the lower part of his body into a fish.

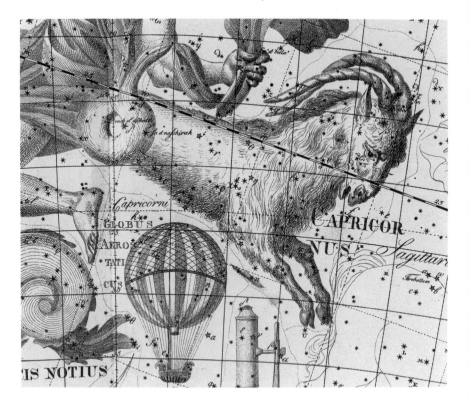

Capricornus as shown in the *Uranographia* of Johann Bode. South of it lies the obsolete constellation of Globus Aerostaticus (see Chapter Four).

Zeus grappled with Typhon, but the monster pulled out the sinews from the hands and feet of Zeus, leaving the god crippled. Hermes and Pan replaced the sinews, allowing Zeus to resume his pursuit of Typhon. Zeus cut down the monster with thunderbolts and finally buried him under Mount Etna in Sicily, which still belches fire from the monster's breath. In gratitude for these services, Zeus placed the image of Pan in the sky as the constellation Capricornus.

The star Alpha Capricorni is variously called Algedi or Giedi, from the Arabic *al-jady* meaning 'the kid', the Arabic name for the constellation. Delta Capricorni is called Deneb Algedi, from the Arabic for 'the kid's tail'. The tropic of Capricorn is the latitude on Earth at which the Sun appears overhead at noon on the winter solstice, around December 22. In Greek times the Sun was in Capricornus on this date, but the effect of precession means that the Sun is now in Sagittarius at the winter solstice.

Carina
— *the keel* —

This is one of the parts into which Argo Navis, the ship of the Argonauts, was divided by the French astronomer Nicolas Louis de Lacaille in his catalogue of the southern stars published in 1763. (For the full story of Argo, see Chapter Four.) Carina represents the ship's keel. It contains the second-brightest star in the entire sky, Canopus, a creamy white supergiant approximately 300 light years away, that marks one of the ship's two steering oars.

Canopus is not mentioned by Aratus, because the star was below the horizon from Greece in his day; the name first appears with Eratosthenes who worked further south, at Alexandria, and hence would have seen the star. Greek writers such as Strabo and Conon tell us that Canopus is named after the helmsman of the Greek King Menelaus. On Menelaus's return from Troy with Helen his fleet was driven off-course by a storm and landed in Egypt. There Canopus died of a snake bite; Helen killed the snake, and she and Menelaus buried Canopus with full honours. On that site grew the city of Canopus (the modern Abu Qir) at the mouth of the Nile. Fittingly, modern space probes now use Canopus as a navigation star. Eratosthenes also knew this star by the name Perigee, in reference to the fact that it remained close to the horizon.

The constellation contains a unique star, Eta Carinae, that flared up to become brighter than Canopus in 1843, but has since sunk to below naked-eye visibility. Astronomers think that it is a young, massive star that will one day explode as a supernova.

— *Cassiopeia* —

Cassiopeia was the vain and boastful wife of King Cepheus of Ethiopia, who lies next to her in the sky. They are the only husband-and-wife couple among the constellations. Classical authors spell her name Cassiepeia, but Cassiopeia is the form used by astronomers.

While combing her long locks one day, Cassiopeia dared to claim that she was more beautiful than the sea nymphs called the Nereids. There were fifty Nereids, daughters of Nereus, the so-called Old Man of the Sea. One of the Nereids, Amphitrite, was married to Poseidon, the sea god. The Nereids appealed to Poseidon to punish Cassiopeia for her vanity, and the sea god sent a monster to ravage the coast of King Cepheus's country. This monster is commemorated in the constellation Cetus. To appease the monster, Cepheus and Cassiopeia chained their daughter Andromeda to a rock as a

Cassiopeia, the vain queen seated on her throne, depicted in the *Atlas Coelestis* of John Flamsteed.

sacrifice, but Andromeda was saved from the monster's jaws by the hero Perseus in one of the most famous rescue stories in history.

As an added punishment, Cassiopeia was condemned to circle the celestial pole for ever, sometimes hanging upside down in undignified posture. In the sky Cassiopeia is depicted sitting on her throne, still fussing with her hair.

The constellation of Cassiopeia has a distinctive W-shape made up of its five brightest stars, which writers such as Aratus likened to a key or a folding door. Alpha Cassiopeiae is called Shedar, from the Arabic meaning 'the breast', which position it marks. Beta Cassiopeia is known as Caph from the Arabic meaning 'stained hand', as it was thought by them to represent a hand stained with henna. Delta Cassiopeiae is named Ruchbah, from the Arabic for 'knee'. The central star of the W, called Gamma Cassiopeiae, is an erratic variable star, given to occasional outbursts in brightness.

Centaurus
— the centaur —

Centaurs were mythical beasts, half-man, half-horse. They were a wild and ill-behaved race, particularly when the wine bottle was opened. But one centaur, Chiron, stood out from the rest as being wise and scholarly, and he is the one who is represented by the constellation Centaurus.

Chiron was born of different parents from the other centaurs, which accounts for his difference in character. His father was Cronus, king of the Titans, who one day caught and seduced the sea nymph Philyra. Surprised in the act by his wife Rhea, Cronus turned himself into a horse and galloped away, leaving Philyra to bear a hybrid son.

Chiron grew up to be a skilled teacher of hunting, medicine and music; his cave on Mount Pelion became a veritable academy for young princes in search of a good education. Chiron was so trusted by the gods and heroes of ancient Greece that he was made foster-father to Jason and Achilles; but perhaps his most successful pupil was Asclepius, son of Apollo, who became the greatest of all healers and is commemorated in the constellation Ophiuchus.

For a creature who did so much good during his lifetime, Chiron suffered a tragic death. It arose from a visit paid by Heracles to the centaur Pholus, who entertained him to dinner and offered him wine from the centaurs' communal jar. When the other centaurs realized their wine was being drunk they burst angrily into the cave, armed with rocks and trees. Heracles repulsed them with a volley of arrows. Some of the centaurs took refuge with Chiron, who had been innocent of the attack, and an arrow of Heracles accidentally struck Chiron in the knee. Heracles, concerned for the good centaur, pulled out the arrow, apologizing profusely, but he already knew that Chiron was doomed. Even Chiron's best medicine was no match for the poison of the Hydra's blood in which Heracles had dipped his arrows.

Aching with pain, but unable to die because he was the immortal son of Cronus, Chiron retreated to his cave. Rather than let him suffer endlessly, Zeus agreed that Chiron should transfer his immortality to Prometheus. Thus released, Chiron died and was placed among the stars. Another

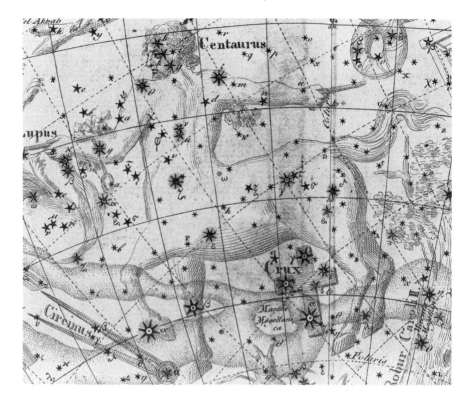

Centaurus from the *Uranographia* of Johann Bode. The centaur holds a long pole on which is impaled Lupus, the wolf. Alpha Centauri, the closest star to the Sun, marks the Centaur's forefoot.

version of the story simply says that Heracles visited Chiron and that while the two were examining his arrows one accidentally dropped on the centaur's foot. In the sky, the centaur is represented as about to sacrifice an animal (the constellation Lupus) on the altar (Ara). Eratosthenes says that this is a sign of Chiron's virtue.

Centaurus contains the closest star to the Sun, Alpha Centauri, 4.3 light years away. Alpha Centauri is also known as Rigil Kentaurus, from the Arabic meaning 'centaur's foot'. To the naked eye it appears as the third-brightest star in the sky, but a small telescope reveals it to be double, consisting of two yellow stars like the Sun. A third, much fainter companion star is called Proxima Centauri because it is slightly closer to us than the other two. Beta Centauri is called Hadar, from an Arabic name signifying one member of a pair of stars. Alpha and Beta Centauri mark the front legs of the centaur, and they act as pointers to Crux, the Southern Cross, which lies under the centaur's rear quarters. Centaurus also contains the largest and brightest globular star cluster visible from Earth, Omega Centauri.

— *Cepheus* —

Cepheus was the mythological king of Ethiopia. He was deemed worthy of a place in the sky because he was fourth in descent from the nymph Io, one of the loves of Zeus – and having Zeus as a relative was always an advantage when it came to being commemorated among the constellations. The kingdom of Cepheus was not the Ethiopia we know today, but stretched from the south-eastern shore of the Mediterranean southwards to the Red Sea, an area that contains parts of the modern Israel, Jordan and Egypt. Ptolemy described him as wearing the tiara-like head-dress of a Persian king.

Cepheus was married to Cassiopeia, an unbearably vain woman whose boastfulness caused Poseidon to send a sea monster, Cetus, to ravage the shores of Cepheus's kingdom. Cepheus was instructed by the Oracle of Ammon to chain his daughter Andromeda to a rock in sacrifice to the monster. She was saved by the hero Perseus, who killed the monster and claimed Andromeda for his bride.

Cepheus in the robes of a Persian king, depicted in the *Atlas Coelestis* of John Flamsteed.

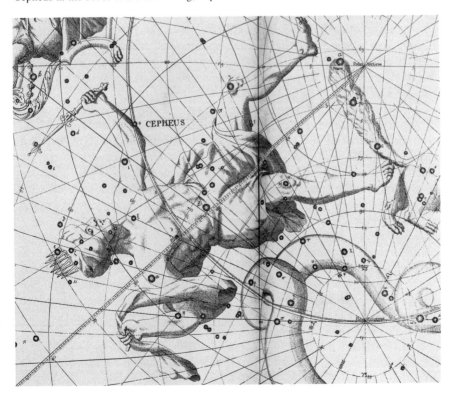

King Cepheus laid on a sumptuous banquet at his palace to celebrate the wedding. But Andromeda had already been promised to Phineus, brother of Cepheus. While the celebrations were in progress, Phineus and his followers burst in, demanding that Andromeda be handed over, which Cepheus refused to do. The dreadful battle that ensued is described in gory detail by Ovid in Book V of his *Metamorphoses*. Cepheus retired from the scene, muttering that he had done his best, and left Perseus to defend himself. Perseus cut down many of his attackers, turning the remainder to stone by showing them the Gorgon's head.

The constellation of Cepheus lies near the north celestial pole. Its most celebrated star is Delta Cephei, a pulsating giant star that varies in brightness every 5.4 days. It is the prototype of the Cepheid variable stars that astronomers use for estimating distances in space.

Cetus
— *the sea monster* —

When Cassiopeia, wife of King Cepheus of Ethiopia, boasted that she was more beautiful than the sea nymphs called the Nereids she set in motion one of the most celebrated stories in mythology, whose characters are commemorated in the sky. In retribution for the insult to the Nereids, the sea god Poseidon sent a monster to ravage the coast of Cepheus's territory. That monster is represented by the constellation Cetus.

To rid himself of the monster, Cepheus was instructed by the Oracle of Ammon to offer up his daughter Andromeda as a sacrifice to the monster. Andromeda was chained to the cliffs at Joppa (the modern Tel-Aviv) to await her terrible fate.

Cetus was visualized by the Greeks as a hybrid creature, with enormous gaping jaws and the forefeet of a land animal, attached to a scaly body with huge coils like a sea serpent. Hence Cetus is drawn on star maps as a most unlikely looking creature, more comical than frightening, nothing like a whale although it is sometimes identified as one.

Andromeda trembled as the B-movie monster made towards her, cleaving through the waves like a huge ship. Fortunately, at this moment the hero Perseus happened by and sized up the situation. Swooping down like an eagle onto the monster's back, Perseus plunged his sword into the creature's right shoulder. The monster reared up on its coils and twisted round, its cruel jaws snapping at its attacker. Again and again Perseus plunged his sword into the beast, through its ribs, its barnacle-encrusted back and at the root of its tail. Spouting blood, the monster finally collapsed into the sea and lay there like a waterlogged hulk. Its corpse was hauled on shore by the appreciative locals, who skinned it and put its bones on display.

Cetus is the fourth-largest constellation, as befits such a monster, but

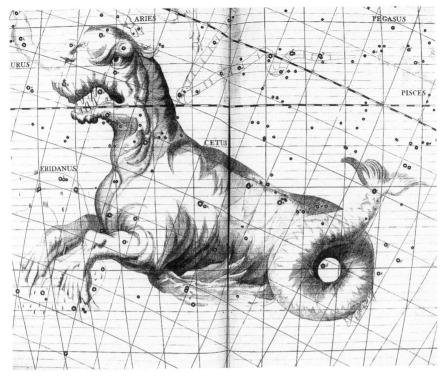

The bizarre-looking sea monster, Cetus, illustrated in the *Atlas Coelestis* of John Flamsteed.

none of its stars is particularly bright. Alpha Ceti is called Menkar from the Arabic meaning 'nostrils', a misnomer since this star lies on the beast's jaw. The most celebrated star in the constellation is Mira, a Latin name meaning 'the amazing one', given on account of its variability in brightness. At times it can be easily seen with the naked eye, but for most of the time it is so faint that it cannot be seen without binoculars or a telescope. Mira is a red giant star whose brightness variations are caused by changes in size. The star was first recorded in 1596 by the Dutch astronomer David Fabricius, but the cyclic nature of the changes was not recognized until 1638. The name Mira was given to the star by the Polish astronomer Johannes Hevelius in 1662, when it was the only variable star known.

Chamaeleon
— *the chameleon* —

The celestial chameleon is one of the constellations representing exotic animals that were introduced by the Dutch navigators Pieter Dirkszoon Keyser and Frederick de Houtman when they charted the southern skies in

1595–97. These new southern constellations were first shown on a globe by the Dutchman Petrus Plancius in 1598 and were rapidly adopted by other map makers such as Johann Bayer, for no other observations of the southern skies were then available. Chamaeleon lies near the south celestial pole. There are no legends associated with it, and it has no bright stars.

Chamaeleon as depicted in the *Uranographia* of Johann Bode.

Circinus
— *the compasses* —

An insignificant constellation representing a pair of compasses used by draughtsmen and navigators. Circinus was introduced in 1756 by the Frenchman Nicolas Louis de Lacaille, who fitted various figures into gaps between the existing constellations of the southern skies. In this case the gap seems to have been almost non-existent, and the compasses are squeezed in their folded position between the forefeet of Centaurus and Triangulum Australe.

Circinus from the *Uranographia* of Johann Bode.

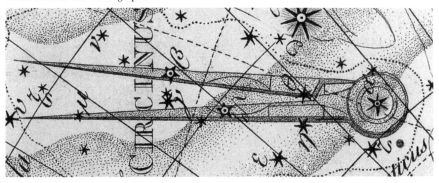

Columba
— the dove —

A constellation formed by the Dutchman Petrus Plancius in 1592, who took some stars that Ptolemy in his *Almagest* had catalogued as being outside Canis Major. Columba lies behind Argo Navis, the ship, which Plancius renamed Noah's Ark. It is supposed to represent Noah's dove, sent out to find dry land. But those familiar with the story of Argo (see Chapter Four) might instead think of it as the dove sent by the Argonauts between the Clashing Rocks to ensure their safe passage. The constellation's brightest star, third-magnitude Alpha Columbae, is called Phact, from an Arabic name meaning 'ring dove'.

Columba shown in the *Uranographia* of Johann Bode.

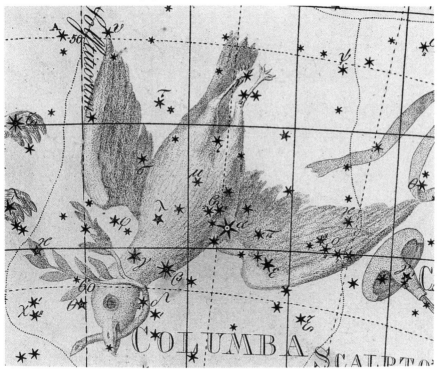

Coma Berenices
— Berenice's hair —

Between Boötes and Leo lies an attractive little swarm of stars that was known to the Greeks, but was not classed by them as a separate constellation, being considered part of Leo. Eratosthenes referred to it as

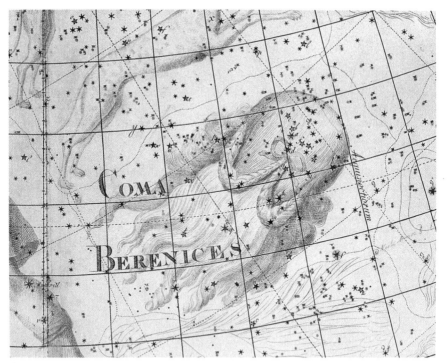

Coma Berenices, the flowing tresses of an Egyptian queen, from the *Uranographia* of Johann Bode.

the hair of Ariadne under his entry on the Northern Crown (Corona Borealis), but under Leo he said it was the hair of Queen Berenice of Egypt, as we know it today. Ptolemy referred to these stars as 'a nebulous mass, called the lock' (i.e. of hair) in his *Almagest* of *c.* AD 150, but the group was officially made into a separate constellation in 1551 by the Dutch cartographer Gerardus Mercator, and in 1602 Tycho Brahe included it in his influential star catalogue.

Berenice was a real person who, in the third century BC, married her brother, Ptolemy III Euergetes, as was the tradition of the Egyptian royal family. Berenice was reputedly a great horsewoman who had already distinguished herself in battle. Hyginus, who deals with the star group under Leo in his *Poetic Astronomy*, tells the following story. It seems that a few days after their marriage Ptolemy set out to attack Asia. Berenice vowed that if he returned victorious she would cut off her hair in gratitude to the gods. On Ptolemy's safe return, the relieved Berenice carried out her promise and placed her hair in the temple dedicated to her mother Arsinoe (identified after her death with Aphrodite) at Zephyrium near the modern Aswan. But the following day the tresses were missing. What really happened to them is not recorded, but Conon of Samos, a mathematician and astronomer who worked at Alexandria, pointed out the group of stars near the tail of the lion, telling the king that the hair of Berenice had gone to join the constellations.

Corona Australis
— *the southern crown* —

Corona Australis was known to the Greeks not as a crown but as a wreath, which is how it is depicted on old star maps. Aratus did not name it as a separate constellation but referred to it as a circlet of stars beneath the forefeet of Sagittarius. Perhaps it has slipped off the archer's head. None of its stars is brighter than fourth magnitude and there seem to be no legends associated with it, unless this is the crown placed in the sky by Dionysus after retrieving his dead mother from the Underworld. Hyginus gives this myth under the Northern Crown (Corona Borealis), but it seems out of place there and he may have confused the two constellations. If so, the wreath would be made of myrtle leaves, for Dionysus left a gift of myrtle in Hades in return for his mother, and the followers of Dionysus wore crowns of myrtle.

Corona Australis, at the forefeet of Sagittarius, in the *Uranographia* of Johann Bode.

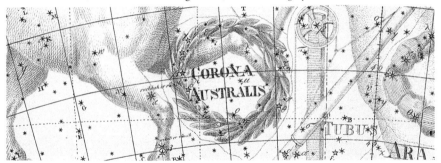

Corona Borealis
— *the northern crown* —

A semi-circle of stars between Boötes and Hercules marks the golden crown worn by Princess Ariadne of Crete when she married the god Dionysus. The crown is said to have been made by Hephaestus, the god of fire, and was studded with jewels from India.

Ariadne, daughter of King Minos of Crete, is famous in mythology for her part in helping Theseus to slay the Minotaur, the gruesome creature with the head of a bull on a human body. Ariadne was actually half-sister to the Minotaur, for her mother Pasiphae had given birth to the creature after copulating with a bull owned by King Minos. To hide the family's shame, Minos imprisoned the Minotaur in a labyrinth designed by the master craftsman Daedalus. So complex was the maze of the labyrinth that neither the Minotaur nor anyone else who ventured in could ever find their way out.

One day the hero Theseus, son of King Aegeus of Athens, came to Crete.

Theseus was a strong, handsome man with many of the qualities of Heracles and was unsurpassed as a wrestler. Ariadne fell in love with him on sight. When Theseus offered to kill the Minotaur she consulted Daedalus, who gave her a ball of thread and advised Theseus to tie one end to the door of the labyrinth and pay out the thread as he went along. After killing the Minotaur with his bare hands, Theseus emerged by following the trail of thread back to the door.

He sailed off with Ariadne, but no sooner had they reached the island of Naxos than he abandoned her. As she sat there, cursing Theseus for his ingratitude, she was seen by Dionysus. The god's heart melted at the sight of the forlorn girl and he married her on the spot.

Accounts differ about where Ariadne's crown came from. One story says that it was given to her by Aphrodite as a wedding present. Others say that Theseus obtained it from the sea nymph Thetis, and that its sparkling light helped Theseus find his way through the labyrinth. Whatever the case, after their wedding Dionysus joyfully tossed the crown into the sky where its jewels changed into stars. Its brightest star is called Gemma, the Latin for 'jewel', though it is also known as Alphecca from the Arabic name for the constellation.

Corona Borealis, a jewelled crown, shown in the *Atlas Coelestis* of John Flamsteed.

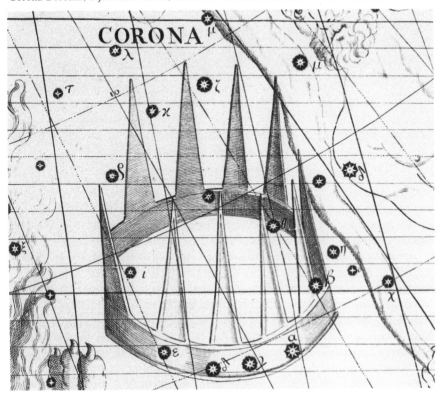

Corvus
— the crow and crater, the cup —

These two adjacent constellations are linked in a moral tale that goes back at least to the time of Eratosthenes. As told by Ovid in his *Fasti*, Apollo was about to make a sacrifice to Zeus and sent the crow to fetch water from a running spring. The crow flew off with a bowl in its claws until it came to a fig tree laden with unripe fruit. Ignoring his orders, the crow waited several days for the fruit to ripen, by which time Apollo had been forced to find a source of water for himself.

After eating his fill of the delicious fruit, the crow looked around for an alibi. He picked up a water-snake in his claws and returned with it to Apollo, saying that the serpent had been blocking the spring. But Apollo, one of whose skills was the art of prophecy, saw through the lie and condemned the crow to a life of thirst – which is perhaps one explanation for the rasping call of the crow. In memorial of this incident, Apollo put the crow, the cup and the water-snake together in the sky.

The crow is depicted pecking at the water-snake's coils, as though attempting to move it so that the crow may reach the cup to drink. The cup,

Corvus and Crater, two adjacent constellations on the back of Hydra, shown in the *Uranographia* of Johann Bode.

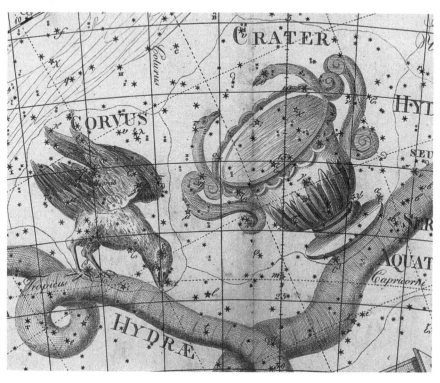

usually represented as a magnificent double-handled chalice, is shown tilted towards the crow but just out of reach of the thirsty bird. The water-snake is the constellation Hydra which, in another legend, doubles as the creature slain by Heracles.

The crow was the sacred bird of Apollo, who changed himself into a crow to flee from the monster Typhon when that immense creature threatened the gods. In another story, related by Ovid in his *Metamorphoses*, the crow was once snow-white like a dove, but the bird brought news to Apollo that his love, Coronis, had been unfaithful. Apollo in his anger cursed the crow, turning it for ever black.

Crux
— *the southern cross* —

This is the smallest of all the eighty-eight constellations. Its stars were known to the ancient Greeks, but were regarded as part of the hind legs of Centaurus, the centaur. The cross itself seems first to have been described in 1516 by the Italian navigator Andreas Corsali, who called it 'so fair and beautiful that no other heavenly sign may be compared to it'. The cross was used by navigators as a pointer to the south celestial pole, and was adopted by astronomers as a separate constellation by the end of the sixteenth century. Crux seems first to appear in its modern form on the celestial globes by the Dutch cartographers Petrus Plancius and Jodocus Hondius in 1598 and 1600 respectively; Plancius had earlier shown a stylized southern cross in a completely different part of the sky, south of Eridanus. The constellation's brightest star is sometimes called Acrux, a name applied by navigators from its scientific designation Alpha Crucis. Through small telescopes it is divisible into two sparkling blue-white points.

Crux lies under the hind legs of Centaurus. It contains a dark cloud of dust known to modern astronomers as the Coalsack, but named Macula Magellanica on this illustration from the *Uranographia* of Johann Bode.

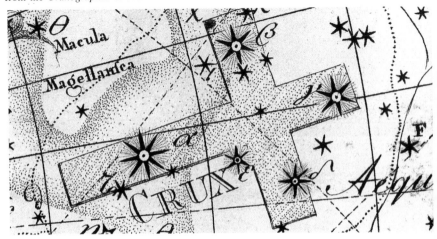

Cygnus
— *the swan* —

A popular name for Cygnus is the Northern Cross, and indeed its shape is far larger and more distinctive than the famous Southern Cross. In its cruciform shape the Greeks visualized the long neck, outstretched wings and stubby tail of a swan flying along the Milky Way, in which it is embedded. The mythographers tell us that the swan is Zeus in disguise, on his way to one of his innumerable love affairs, but his exact target is a subject of some disagreement.

Cygnus flying down the Milky Way in a chart from the *Atlas Coelestis* of John Flamsteed. At the root of its tail lies the bright star Deneb, here labelled Alpha.

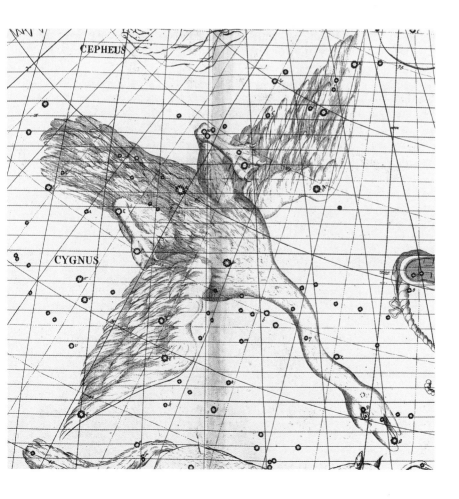

The version of the tale that goes back to Eratosthenes says that Zeus one day took a fancy to the nymph Nemesis, who lived at Rhamnus, some way north-east of Athens. To escape his unwelcome advances she assumed the form of various animals, first jumping into a river, then fleeing across land and finally taking flight as a goose. Not to be outdone, Zeus pursued her through all these transformations, at each step turning himself into a larger and swifter animal, until he finally became a swan in which form he caught and raped her. Hyginus tells a similar story, but does not mention the metamorphoses of Nemesis. Rather, he says that Zeus pretended to be a swan escaping from an eagle and that Nemesis gave the swan sanctuary. Only after she had gone to sleep with the swan in her lap did she discover her mistake.

In both versions the outcome was that Nemesis produced an egg which was then given to Queen Leda of Sparta, some say by Hermes and others say by a passing shepherd who found the egg in a wood. Out of the egg hatched the beautiful Helen (later to become famous as Helen of Troy).

A simpler version says that Zeus seduced Leda in the form of a swan by the banks of the river Eurotas; with this story in mind, Germanicus Caesar refers to the swan as the 'winged adulterer'. Leda was the wife of King Tyndareus of Sparta, which considerably complicated the outcome because she also slept with her husband later that same night.

According to one interpretation, she gave birth to a single egg from which hatched the twins Castor and Polydeuces as well as Helen. The shell of this egg was said to have been put on display at a temple in Sparta, hanging by ribbons from the roof. A rival account says that Leda produced two eggs, from one of which emerged Castor and Polydeuces while from the other came Helen and her sister Clytemnestra. To add to the confusion, Polydeuces and Helen were reputedly the children of Zeus, while Castor and Clytemnestra were fathered by Tyndareus. Castor and Polydeuces are commemorated by the constellation Gemini, where Polydeuces is better known to astronomers by his Latin name, Pollux.

Cygnus's brightest star, Deneb, marks the tail of the swan; its name comes from *dhanab*, the Arabic word for 'tail'. The Greeks had no name for this prominent star. Deneb is a highly luminous supergiant star, nearly 2000 light years away, the most distant of all first-magnitude stars. It forms one corner of the so-called Summer Triangle of stars completed by Vega in the constellation Lyra and Altair in Aquila.

The beak of the swan is marked by a star named Albireo, revealed by small telescopes to be a beautiful coloured double star of green and amber, like a celestial traffic light. The German historian Paul Kunitzsch has traced the tortuous history of the name Albireo. It started with an Arabic translation of the Greek word for 'bird', *ornis*, the name by which both Aratus and Ptolemy knew the constellation. In the Middle Ages this Arabic name was mistranslated back into Latin, where it was described as *ab ireo*, meaning that it was thought to come from the name of a certain herb. This phrase was itself mistaken for an Arabic name and was rewritten as *albireo*.

Hence the name Albireo, although it looks Arabic, is completely meaning-less.

Cygnus lies in the Milky Way and hence contains many attractive star fields for sweeping with binoculars. Its most celebrated object cannot be seen by optical means at all: a black hole, called Cygnus X-1 because it is a strong source of X-rays, which lies near the middle of the swan's neck.

Delphinus
— the dolphin —

Dolphins were a familiar sight to Greek sailors, so it is not surprising to find one of these friendly and intelligent creatures depicted in the sky. Two stories account for the presence of the celestial dolphin. According to Eratosthenes, this dolphin represents the messenger of the sea god Poseidon.

After Zeus, Poseidon and Hades had overthrown their father Cronus, they divided up the sky, the sea and the underworld between them, with Poseidon inheriting the sea. He built himself a magnificent underwater palace off the island of Euboea. For all its opulence, the palace felt empty without a wife, so Poseidon set out in search of one. He courted Amphitrite, one of the group of sea nymphs called Nereids, but she fled from his rough advances and took refuge among the other Nereids. Poseidon sent messengers after her, including a dolphin, which found her and with soothing gestures brought her back to the sea god, whom she subsequently married. In gratitude, Poseidon placed the image of the dolphin among the stars.

Another story, given by Hyginus and Ovid, says that this is the dolphin that saved the life of Arion, a real-life poet and musician of the seventh century BC. Arion was born on the island of Lesbos, but his reputation spread throughout Greece for he was said to be unequalled in his skill with the lyre. While Arion was returning to Greece by ship from a concert tour of Sicily, the sailors plotted to kill him and steal the small fortune that he had earned. When the sailors surrounded him with swords drawn, Arion asked to be allowed to sing one last song. His music attracted a school of dolphins which swam alongside the ship, leaping playfully. Placing his faith in the gods, Arion leaped overboard – and one of the dolphins carried him on its back to Greece, where Arion later confronted his attackers and had them sentenced to death. Apollo, god of music and poetry, placed the dolphin among the constellations, along with the lyre of Arion which is represented by the constellation Lyra.

Two stars in Delphinus bear the peculiar names of Sualocin and Rotanev, given to them in 1814 by the Italian astronomer Niccolo Cacciatore, assistant and successor to the great Giuseppe Piazzi at Palermo Observatory. Read backwards, the names spell out Nicolaus Venator, the Latinized form of Niccolo Cacciatore. He is the only person to have named a star after himself and got away with it.

Delphinus as shown in the *Atlas Coelestis* of John Flamsteed.

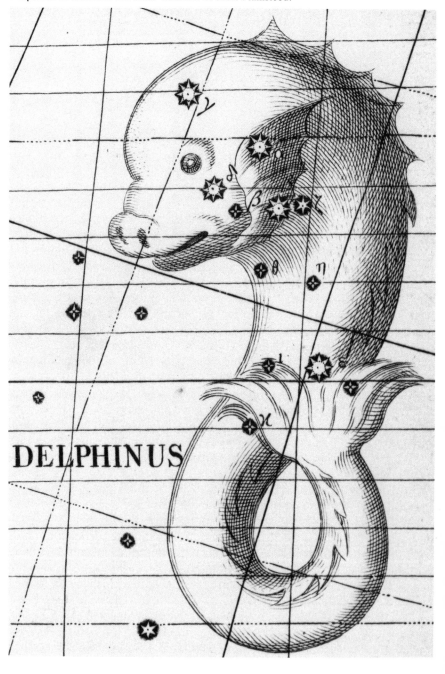

DELPHINUS

Dorado
— *the goldfish* —

A small southern constellation introduced at the end of the sixteenth century by the Dutch navigators Pieter Dirkszoon Keyser and Frederick de Houtman. Dorado was first depicted on a star globe of 1598 by the Dutchman Petrus Plancius. The constellation has also been known as Xiphias, the Swordfish, which is how it was depicted on the star atlas of Johann Bode. Dorado's main claim to fame is that it contains most of the Large Magellanic Cloud, a small neighbour galaxy of our own Milky Way, about 160,000 light years away.

Dorado shown in the *Uranographia* of Johann Bode as Xiphias, the swordfish. Nubecula Major is the Large Magellanic Cloud.

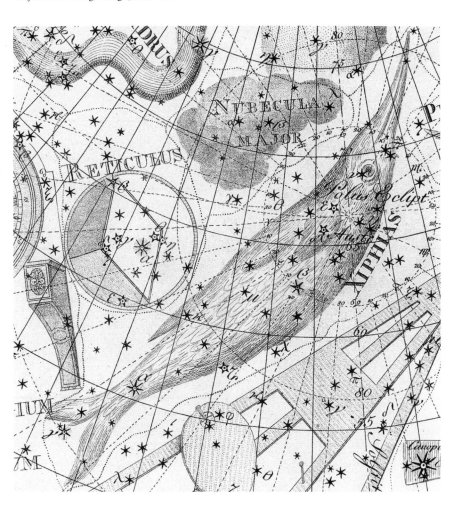

Draco
— *the dragon* —

Coiled around the sky's north pole is the celestial dragon, Draco. Legend has it that this is the dragon slain by Heracles during one of his labours, and in the sky the dragon is depicted with one foot of Heracles (in the form of the neighbouring constellation Hercules) upon its head. This dragon, named

Draco winding around the north celestial pole in the *Uranographia* of Johann Bode. The dragon's long tail is labelled Cauda Draconis.

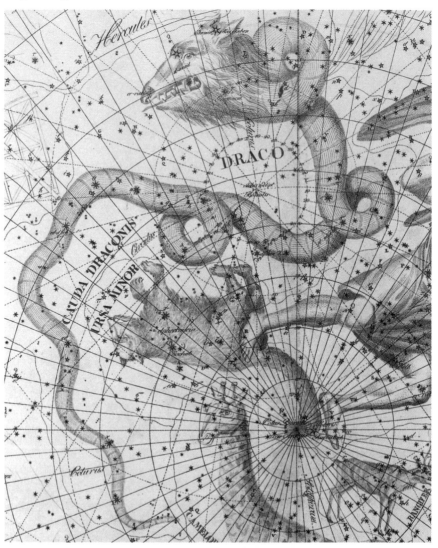

Ladon, guarded the precious tree on which grew golden apples.

Hera had been given the golden apple tree as a wedding present when she married Zeus. She was so delighted with it that she planted it in her garden on the slopes of Mount Atlas and set the Hesperides, daughters of Atlas, to guard it. Most authorities say there were three Hesperides, but Apollodorus names four. They proved untrustworthy guards, for they kept picking the apples. Sterner measures were required, so Hera placed the dragon Ladon around the tree to ward off pilferers.

According to Apollodorus, Ladon was the offspring of the monster Typhon and Echidna, a creature half woman and half serpent. Ladon had one hundred heads, says Apollodorus, and could talk in different voices. Hesiod, though, says that the dragon was the offspring of the sea deities Phorcys and Ceto, and he does not mention the number of heads. In the sky, the dragon is shown with one head.

The great hero Heracles was required to steal some apples from the tree as one of his labours. He did so by killing the dragon with his poisoned arrows. According to Apollonius Rhodius, the Argonauts came across the body of Ladon the day after Heracles had shot him. The dragon lay by the trunk of the apple tree, its tail still twitching but the rest of its coiled body bereft of life. Flies died in the poison of its festering wounds while nearby the Hesperides bewailed the dragon's death, covering their golden heads with their white arms. Hera placed the image of the dragon in the sky as the constellation Draco.

Despite its considerable size, the eighth-largest constellation, Draco is not particularly prominent. Its brightest star is second-magnitude Gamma Draconis, called Eltanin, from the Arabic *al-tinnin* meaning 'the serpent'. Alpha Draconis is called Thuban, from a highly corrupted form of the Arabic *ra's al-tinnin*, 'the serpent's head'. Beta Draconis is called Rastaban, another corrupted form of the same Arabic name.

Equuleus
— *the little horse* —

This insignificant constellation, second-smallest in the sky, first appeared among the forty-eight constellations listed by the Greek astronomer Ptolemy in the second century AD. It was unknown to Aratus 400 years earlier. The actual inventor of Equuleus is unknown; it may have been Ptolemy himself or one of his predecessors such as Hipparchus in the second century BC.

Equuleus consists merely of a few stars of fourth magnitude and fainter forming the head of a horse, next to the head of the much better-known horse Pegasus. The early mythologists such as Eratosthenes and Hyginus never mentioned this little horse, but perhaps Ptolemy had in mind the story of Hippe and her daughter Melanippe, sometimes told for Pegasus but which seems more appropriate for Equuleus.

Hippe, daughter of Chiron the centaur, one day was seduced by Aeolus, grandson of Deucalion. To hide the secret of her pregnancy from Chiron she fled into the mountains, where she gave birth to Melanippe. When her father came looking for her, Hippe appealed to the gods who changed her into a mare. Artemis placed the image of Hippe among the stars, where she still hides from Chiron (the constellation Centaurus), with only her head showing.

The fourth-magnitude star Alpha Equulei is called Kitalpha from the Arabic meaning 'the section of the horse', in reference to the whole constellation. For illustration, see Pegasus.

Eridanus
— *the river* —

Early writers seem to have regarded the Eridanus as a mythical river, flowing into the great Ocean that surrounded the lands of the known world. Virgil called it 'the king of rivers'. Eratosthenes identified it as the Nile, 'the only river which runs from south to north'. Hyginus agreed with this identification, pointing out that the star Canopus (marking a steering oar of the ship Argo) lay at the end of the celestial river, as the island Canopus lies at the mouth of the Nile. But Hesiod in his *Theogony* listed the Nile and Eridanus separately, showing that he regarded them as different rivers. Later Greek writers identified the Eridanus with the river Po in Italy.

In mythology, the Eridanus features in the story of Phaethon, son of the Sun-god Helios, who begged to be allowed to drive his father's chariot across the sky. Reluctantly Helios agreed to the request, but warned Phaethon of the dangers he was facing. 'Follow the track across the heavens where you will see my wheel marks', Helios advised.

As Dawn threw open her doors in the east, Phaethon enthusiastically mounted the Sun-god's golden chariot studded with glittering jewels, little knowing what he was letting himself in for. The four horses immediately noticed the lightness of the chariot with its different rider and they bolted upwards into the sky, off the beaten track, with the chariot bobbing around like a poorly ballasted ship behind them. Even had Phaethon known where the true path lay, he lacked the skill and the strength to control the reins.

The team galloped northwards, so that for the first time the stars of the Plough grew hot and Draco, the dragon, which until then had been sluggish with the cold, sweltered in the heat and snarled furiously. Looking down on Earth from the dizzying heights, the panic-stricken Phaethon grew pale and his knees trembled in fear. Finally, he saw the constellation of the Scorpion with its huge claws outstretched and its poisonous tail raised to strike.

Eridanus meanders across this chart from Johann Bode's *Uranographia*. At upper right are the flippers of Cetus, and below them lies Apparatus Chemicus, the name given by Bode to the constellation now known as Fornax.

Young Phaethon let the reins slip from his grasp and the horses galloped out of control.

Ovid graphically describes Phaethon's crazy ride in Book II of his *Metamorphoses*. The chariot plunged so low that the Earth caught fire. Enveloped in hot smoke, Phaethon was swept along by the horses, not knowing where he was. It was then, the mythologists say, that Libya became a desert, the Ethiopians acquired their dark skins and the seas dried up. To bring the catastrophic events to an end, Zeus struck Phaethon down with a thunderbolt. With his hair streaming fire, the youth plunged like a shooting star into the Eridanus. Some time later, when the Argonauts sailed up the river, they found his body still smouldering, sending up clouds of foul-smelling steam in which birds choked and died.

Eridanus is a long constellation, the sixth-largest in the sky, meandering from the foot of Orion far into the southern hemisphere, ending near Tucana, the Toucan. The constellation's brightest star, first-magnitude Alpha Eridani, is called Achernar, from the Arabic meaning 'the river's end'; it does indeed mark the southern end of Eridanus.

Fornax
— *the furnace* —

An obscure constellation introduced by the Frenchman Nicolas Louis de Lacaille after his trip to the Cape of Good Hope to observe the southern stars in 1751–52. Fornax represents a chemist's furnace, Bode showed it in on his atlas as Apparatus Chemicus. Fornax contains no stars brighter than fourth magnitude and none of them are named.

Gemini
— *the twins* —

Gemini represents the twins Castor and Polydeuces (Pollux is the Latin form of his name); they were known to the Greeks as the Dioscuri, literally meaning 'sons of Zeus'. However, mythologists disputed whether both really were sons of Zeus, because of the unusual circumstances of their birth. Their mother was Leda, Queen of Sparta, whom Zeus visited one day in the form of a swan (represented by the constellation Cygnus). That same night she also slept with her husband, King Tyndareus. Both unions were fruitful, for Leda subsequently gave birth to four children. In the most commonly accepted version, Polydeuces and Helen (later to become famous as Helen of Troy) were children of Zeus, and hence immortal, while Castor and Clytemnestra were fathered by Tyndareus, and hence were mortal.

Castor and Polydeuces grew up the closest of friends, never quarrelling or acting without consulting each other. They were said to look alike and even to dress alike, as identical twins often do. Castor was a famed horseman and warrior who taught Heracles to fence, while Polydeuces was a champion boxer.

The inseparable twins joined the expedition of Jason and the Argonauts in search of the golden fleece. The boxing skills of Polydeuces came in use when the Argonauts landed in a region of Asia Minor ruled by Amycus, a son of Poseidon. Amycus, the world's greatest bully, would not allow visitors to leave until they had fought him in a boxing match, which he

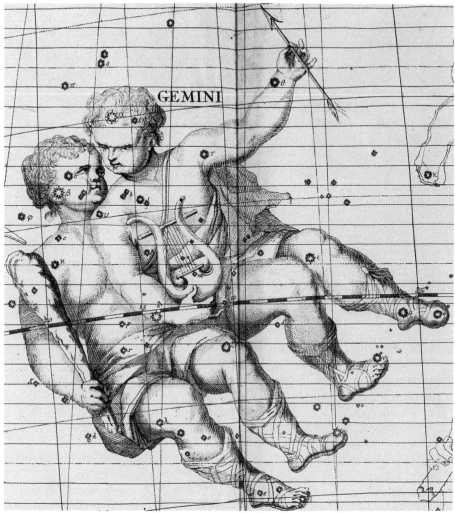

The inseparable twins Castor and Polydeuces are commemorated in the constellation Gemini, depicted here in the *Atlas Coelestis* of John Flamsteed. Castor carries a lyre and an arrow, Polydeuces a club. The stars Castor and Pollux mark the heads of the twins.

invariably won. He stamped down to the shore where the Argo lay and challenged the crew to put up a man against him. Polydeuces, stirred by the man's arrogance, accepted at once and the two pulled on leather gloves. Polydeuces easily avoided the rushes of his opponent, like a matador side-stepping a charging bull, and felled Amycus with a blow to the head that splintered his skull.

On the Argonauts' homeward trip with the golden fleece Castor and Polydeuces were of further value to the crew. Apollonius Rhodius tells us briefly that during the voyage from the mouth of the Rhone to the Stoechades Islands (the present-day Iles d'Hyères off Toulon) the Argonauts owed their safety to Castor and Polydeuces. Presumably a storm was involved, but he does not elaborate on the circumstances. Ever since this episode, says Apollonius – and he assures us there were other voyages on which they were saviours – the twins have been the patron saints of sailors. Hyginus said that the twins were given the power to save shipwrecked sailors by Poseidon, the sea god, who also presented them with the white horses that they often rode.

Mariners believed that during storms at sea the twins appeared in a ship's rigging in the form of the electrical phenomenon known as St Elmo's fire, as described by Pliny, the Roman writer of the first century AD, in his book *Natural History*:

> On a voyage stars alight on the yards and other parts of the ship. If there are two of them, they denote safety and portend a successful voyage. For this reason they are called Castor and Pollux, and people pray to them as gods for aid at sea.

A single glow was called a Helen and was considered a sign of disaster.

Castor and Polydeuces clashed with another pair of twins, Idas and Lynceus, over two beautiful women. Idas and Lynceus (who were also members of the Argo's crew) were engaged to Phoebe and Hilaira, but Castor and Polydeuces carried them off. Idas and Lynceus gave pursuit and the two sets of twins fought it out. Castor was run through by a sword thrust from Lynceus, whereupon Polydeuces killed him. Idas attacked Polydeuces but was repulsed by a thunderbolt from Zeus.

Another story says that the two pairs of twins made up their quarrel over the women, but came to blows over the division of some cattle they had jointly rustled. Whatever the case, Polydeuces grieved for his fallen brother and asked Zeus that the two should share immortality. Zeus placed them both in the sky as the constellation Gemini, where they are seen in close embrace, inseparable to the last.

Aratus referred to the constellation only as the Twins, without identifying them, but Eratosthenes named them as Castor and Polydeuces. An alternative view, reported by Hyginus, says that the constellation represents Apollo and Heracles, both sons of Zeus but not twins. Ptolemy supported this interpretation; the stars that we know as Castor and Pollux he called 'the star of Apollo' and 'the star of Heracles'. This identification is found not in Ptolemy's famous *Almagest* but in a more obscure treatise called *Tetrabiblos*, about astrology. Several star maps personify the twins as Apollo and Heracles; on the illustration shown here, for instance, one twin is depicted holding a lyre and arrow, attributes of Apollo, while the other carries a club, as did Heracles.

The two brightest stars in the constellation are named Castor and Pollux, marking the heads of the twins. Astronomers have found that Castor is actually a complex system of six stars linked by gravity. Pollux is an orange giant star. Unlike the twins that they represent, the stars Castor and Pollux are not related since they lie at different distances from us. Eta Geminorum is called Propus, meaning 'forward foot' in Greek, a name that first appears with Eratosthenes.

Grus
— *the crane* —

One of the twelve constellations introduced at the end of the sixteenth century by the Dutch navigators Pieter Dirkszoon Keyser and Frederick de Houtman after their pioneer mapping of the southern skies. Grus represents

Grus depicted in the *Uranographia* of Johann Bode.

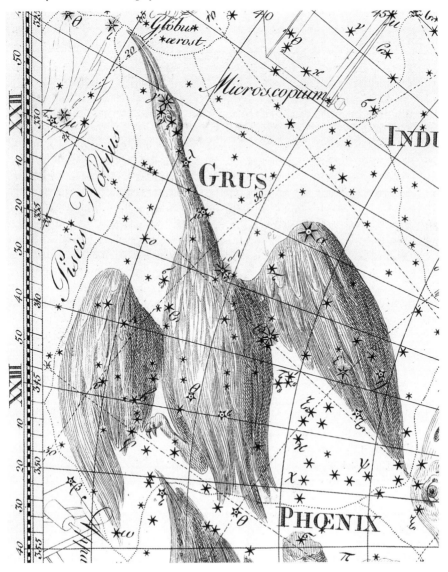

a long-necked bird, the crane. The constellation was first shown on a celestial globe by Petrus Plancius in 1598, although on a later globe Plancius gave it the alternative name of Phoenicopterus, the Flamingo. Grus was formed from stars underneath Piscis Austrinus, the Southern Fish. The constellation's brightest star, of second magnitude, is named Alnair, from an abbreviation of the Arabic meaning 'the bright one from the fish's tail', for the Arabs had extended the tail of the southern fish into this region. There are no legends associated with Grus, but in mythology the crane was sacred to Hermes.

— *Hercules* —

The origin of this constellation is so ancient that its true identity was lost even to the Greeks who knew the figure simply as Engonasin, literally meaning 'the kneeling one'. The Greek poet Aratus described him as being worn out with toil, his hands upraised, with one knee bent and a foot on the head of Draco, the dragon. 'No one knows his name, nor what he labours at', said Aratus. But Eratosthenes, a century after Aratus, identified the figure as Heracles (the Greek name for Hercules) triumphing over the dragon that guarded the golden apples of the Hesperides. The Greek playwright Aeschylus, quoted by Hyginus, offered a different explanation. He said that Heracles was kneeling, wounded and exhausted, during his battle with the Ligurians.

Heracles is the greatest of Greek and Roman heroes, the equivalent of the Sumerian hero Gilgamesh. So it is surprising that the Greeks allotted him a constellation only as an afterthought. One reason may be that he was already sometimes personified as one of the heavenly twins represented by the constellation Gemini, the other twin being Apollo.

The full saga of Heracles is long and complex, as befits a legend that has grown in the telling. Heracles was the illicit son of the god Zeus and Alcmene, most beautiful and wise of mortal women, whom Zeus visited in the form of her husband, Amphitryon. He was christened Alcides, Alcaeus or even Palaemon, according to different accounts; the name Heracles came later. Zeus's real wife, Hera, was furious at her husband's infidelity. Worse still, Zeus laid the infant Heracles at Hera's breast while she slept, so that he suckled her milk. And having drunk the milk of a goddess, Heracles became immortal.

As Heracles grew up he surpassed all other men in size, strength and skills with weapons, but he was for ever dogged by the jealousy of Hera. She could not kill him, since he was immortal, so instead she vowed to make his life as unpleasant as possible. Under Hera's evil spell he killed his children in a fit of madness. When sanity returned, he went remorsefully to the Oracle at Delphi to ask how he might atone for his dreadful deed. The Oracle

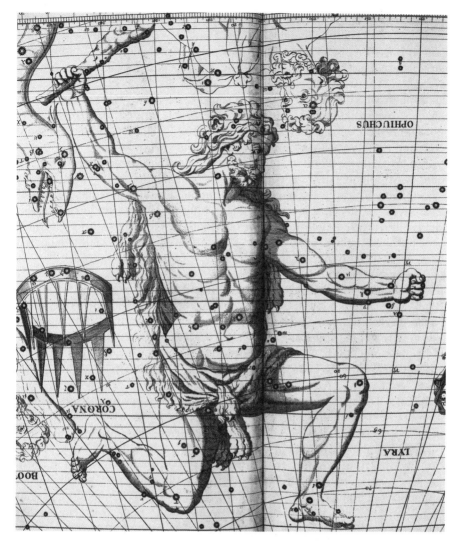

Hercules, the kneeling man, from the *Atlas Coelestis* of John Flamsteed. He wears a lion's skin and carries a club, his favourite weapon. Here his left hand is empty, but other illustrations show it grasping either the three-headed Cerberus or an apple branch.

ordered him to serve Eurystheus, king of Mycenae, for twelve years. It was then that the Oracle gave him the name Heracles, meaning 'glory of Hera'.

Eurystheus set him a series of ten tasks that are called the Labours of Heracles. The first was to kill a lion that was terrorizing the land around the city of Nemea. This lion had a hide that was impervious to any weapons – so Heracles strangled it to death. He used its own claws to cut off the skin. Thereafter he wore the pelt of the lion as a cloak, with its gaping mouth as a helmet, which made him look even more formidable. The Nemean lion is identified with the constellation Leo.

The second labour was to destroy the multi-headed monster called the

Hydra which lurked in the swamp near the town of Lerna, devouring incautious passers-by. Heracles grappled with the monster, but as soon as he cut off one of its heads, two grew to replace it. To make matters worse, a large crab came scuttling out of the swamp and attacked the feet of Heracles. Angrily he stamped on the crab and called for help to Iolaus, his charioteer, who burned the stumps as each head was lopped to prevent more heads growing. Heracles gutted the Hydra and dipped his arrows in its poisonous blood – an action that would eventually be his undoing. Both the crab and the Hydra are commemorated as constellations.

For his next two labours, Heracles was ordered to catch elusive animals: a deer with golden horns, and a ferocious boar. Perhaps the most famous labour is his fifth, the cleaning of the dung-filled stables of King Augeias of Elis. Heracles struck a bargain with the king that he would clean out the stables in a single day in return for one-tenth of the king's cattle. Heracles accomplished the task by diverting two rivers. But Augeias, claiming he had been tricked, renounced the bargain and banished Heracles from Elis.

The next task took him to the town of Stymphalus where he dispersed a flock of marauding birds with arrow-like feathers. The survivors flew to the Black Sea, where they subsequently attacked Jason and the Argonauts. Next, Heracles sailed to Crete to capture a fire-breathing bull that was ravaging the land. Some equate this bull with the constellation Taurus. For his eighth and ninth labours, Heracles brought to Eurystheus the flesh-eating horses of King Diomedes of Thrace and the belt of Hippolyte, queen of the Amazons.

Finally, Heracles was sent to steal the cattle of Geryon, a triple-bodied monster who ruled the island of Erytheia, far to the west. While sailing there, Heracles set up the columns at the straits of Gibraltar called the Pillars of Heracles. He killed Geryon with a single arrow that pierced all three bodies from the side, then drove the cattle back to Greece. On route through Liguria, in southern France, he was set upon by local forces who so outnumbered him that he ran out of arrows. Sinking to his knees, he prayed to his father, Zeus, who rained down rocks on the plain. Heracles hurled these rocks at his attackers and routed them. According to Aeschylus, this is the incident that is recorded by the constellation Engonasin.

When Heracles returned from the last of these exploits, the cowardly and deceitful Eurystheus refused to release him from his service because Heracles had been given help in slaying the Hydra and had attempted to profit from the stable-cleaning. Hence Eurystheus set two additional tasks, more difficult than any before. The first was to steal the golden apples from the garden of Hera on the slopes of Mount Atlas. The tree with the golden fruit was a wedding present from Mother Earth (Gaia) when Hera married Zeus. Hera set the Hesperides, daughters of Atlas, to guard the tree, but they stole some of the golden fruit. So now the dragon Ladon lay coiled around the tree to prevent any further pilfering.

After a heroic journey, during which he released Prometheus from his bonds, Heracles came to the garden where the golden apples grew. Nearby stood Atlas, supporting the heavens on his shoulders. Heracles dispatched Ladon with a well-aimed arrow, and Hera set the dragon in the sky as the constellation Draco. Heracles had been advised (by Prometheus, says Apollodorus) not to pick the apples himself, so he invited Atlas to fetch them for him while he temporarily supported the skies. Heracles hastily returned the burden of the skies to the shoulders of Atlas before making off with the golden treasure.

The twelfth labour, the most daunting of all, took him down to the the gates of the Underworld to fetch Cerberus, the three-headed watchdog. Cerberus had the tail of a dragon and his back was covered with snakes. A more loathsome creature would be difficult to imagine but Heracles, protected from the tail and the snakes by the skin of the Nemean lion, wrestled Cerberus with his bare hands and dragged the slavering dog to Eurystheus. The startled king had never expected to see Heracles alive again. Now, with all the labours completed, Eurystheus had no option but to make Heracles a free man again.

The death of Heracles is a piece of true Greek tragedy. After his labours, Heracles married Deianeira, the young and beautiful daughter of King Oeneus. While travelling together, Heracles and Deianeira came to the swollen river Evenus where the centaur Nessus ferried passengers across. Heracles swam across himself, leaving Deianeira to be carried by Nessus. The centaur, inflamed by her beauty, tried to ravish her, and Heracles shot him with one of his arrows tipped with the Hydra's poison.

The dying centaur offered Deianeira some of his blood, deceitfully saying that it would act as a love charm. Innocently, Deianeira accepted the poisoned blood and kept it safely until, much later, she began to suspect that Heracles had his eye on another woman. In the hope of rekindling his affection, Deianeira gave Heracles a shirt on which she had smeared the blood of the dying Nessus. Heracles put it on – and as the blood warmed up, the Hydra's poison began to burn his flesh to the bone.

In agony, Heracles raged over the countryside, tearing up trees. Realizing there was no release from the pain, he built himself a funeral pyre on Mount Oeta, spread out his lion's skin and lay down on it, peaceful at last. The flames burned up the mortal part of him, and the immortal part ascended to join the gods on Mount Olympus. His father, Zeus, turned him into a constellation.

Heracles is depicted in the sky holding his club, his favourite weapon. Some people think that his twelve labours are represented by the twelve signs of the zodiac, but it is difficult to see the connection in some cases.

Hercules is the fifth-largest constellation, but is not particularly prominent. Alpha Herculis, a red giant star that varies from third to fourth magnitude, is called Rasalgethi, from the Arabic meaning 'the kneeler's head'. The most celebrated object in the constellation is a globular cluster of stars, M13, the best example of such a cluster in northern skies.

Horologium
— the pendulum clock —

One of the small southern constellations introduced by the Frenchman
Nicolas Louis de Lacaille after he mapped the southern stars in 1751–52. As
can be seen from the illustration, the clock was imagined with a fully marked
dial and even a second-hand, a remarkable feat for an area of sky that
contains a sparse scattering of stars no brighter than fourth magnitude.

Horologium illustrated in the *Uranographia* of Johann Bode.

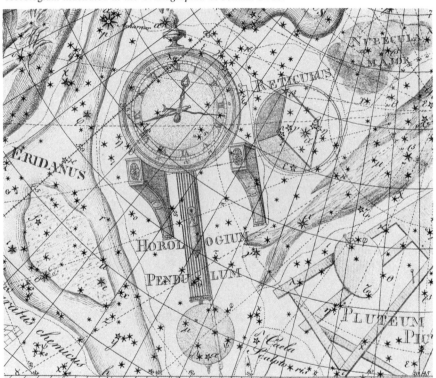

Hydra
— the water-snake —

Hydra is the largest of the eighty-eight constellations, winding a quarter of
the way around the sky. Its head is south of the constellation of Cancer, the
Crab, while the tip of its tail lies between Libra, the Scales, and Centaurus,
the Centaur. Yet despite its size there is nothing prominent about Hydra. Its
only star of note is second-magnitude Alphard, a name that comes from the
Arabic *al-fard* appropriately meaning 'the solitary one'.

The water-snake features in two legends. First, and most familiar, the
Hydra was the creature that Heracles fought and killed as the second of his

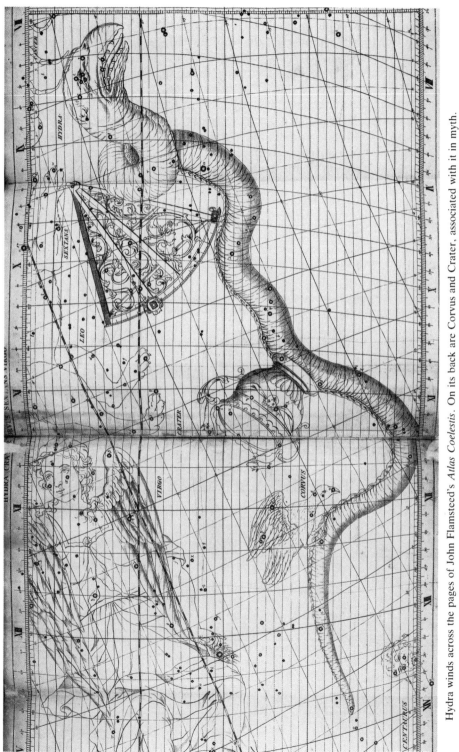

Hydra winds across the pages of John Flamsteed's *Atlas Coelestis*. On its back are Corvus and Crater, associated with it in myth.

famous labours. The Hydra was a multi-headed creature, the offspring of the monster Typhon and the half-woman, half-serpent called Echidna. Hydra was thus the brother of the dragon that guarded the golden apples, commemorated in the constellation Draco. Hydra reputedly had nine heads, the middle one of which was immortal. (In the sky, though, it is shown with one head only – perhaps this is the immortal one.)

Hydra lived in a swamp near the town of Lerna, from where it sallied forth over the surrounding plain, eating cattle and ravaging the countryside. Its breath and even the smell of its tracks were said to be so poisonous that anyone who breathed them died in agony.

Heracles rode up to the Hydra's lair in his chariot and fired flaming arrows into the swamp to force the creature into the open, where he grappled with it. The Hydra wrapped itself around one of his legs; Heracles smashed at its heads with his club, but no sooner had one head been destroyed than two grew in its place. To add to Heracles's worries, a huge crab scuttled out of the swamp and atacked his other foot, but Heracles stamped on the crab and crushed it. The crab is commemorated in the constellation Cancer.

Heracles called for help to his charioteer Iolaus who burned the stump of each head as soon as it was struck off to prevent others growing in its place. Finally Heracles cut off the immortal head of the Hydra and buried it under a heavy rock by the roadside. He slit open the body of the Hydra and dipped his arrows in its poisonous gall.

A second legend associates the water-snake with the constellations of the Crow (Corvus) and the Cup (Crater) that lie on its back. In this story, the crow was sent by Apollo to fetch water in the bowl, but loitered to eat figs from a tree. When the crow eventually returned to Apollo it blamed the water-snake for blocking the spring. But Apollo knew that the crow was lying, and punished him by placing him in the sky, where the water-snake eternally prevents him from drinking out of the bowl.

Hydrus
— *the little water-snake* —

A small southern counterpart of the great water-snake, Hydra, with which it is not to be confused. This is one of several examples of the repetition of constellation figures in the sky, as in the Great and Little Bear, the Great and Little Dog, the two lions, the horses Pegasus and Equuleus, the Northern and Southern Crown and the Northern and Southern Triangle. Hydrus was one of the twelve constellations introduced at the end of the sixteenth century by the Dutch navigators Pieter Dirkszoon Keyser and Frederick de Houtman. Hydrus snakes between the two Magellanic Clouds. The constellation's brightest stars are of third magnitude, but none are named.

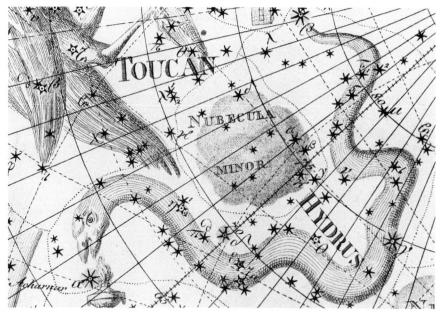

Hydrus shown by Johann Bode in his *Uranographia*. Nubecula Minor is the Small Magnellanic Cloud.

Indus
— *the indian* —

This constellation, representing an American native Indian, is one of the twelve figures formed by the Dutch navigators Pieter Dirkszoon Keyser and Frederick de Houtman from stars they charted in the southern hemisphere at the end of the sixteenth century. The Indian is depicted holding spears or arrows as though hunting. The constellation's brightest stars are of third magnitude, but none are named.

Indus, an Indian holding a spear, shown by Johann Bode in his *Uranographia*.

Lacerta
— *the lizard* —

This inconspicuous constellation, sandwiched between Cygnus and Andromeda, was introduced by the Polish astronomer Johannes Hevelius on his star atlas *Firmamentum Sobiescianum* in 1687. Hevelius also gave it the alternative title of Stellio, the Newt, which soon fell into disuse. Lacerta's stars are of fourth magnitude and fainter and none have names, nor are there any legends associated with the constellation.

Lacerta shown in the *Uranographia* of Johann Bode.

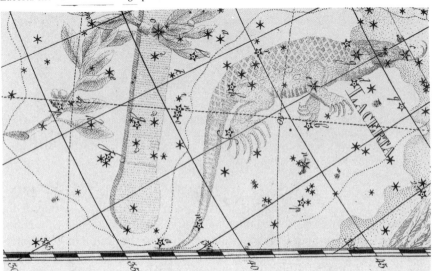

Leo
— *the lion* —

Eratosthenes and Hyginus affirm that the lion was placed in the sky because it is the king of beasts. Mythologically speaking, it is reputed to be the lion of Nemea, slain by Heracles as the first of his twelve labours. Nemea is a town some way south-west of Corinth. There the lion lived in a cave with two mouths, emerging to carry off the local inhabitants, who were becoming scarce. The lion was an invulnerable beast of uncertain parentage; it was variously said to have been sired by the dog Orthrus, the monster Typhon or even to be the offspring of Selene, the Moon goddess. Its skin was proof against all weapons, as Heracles found when he shot an arrow at the lion and saw that it simply bounced off.

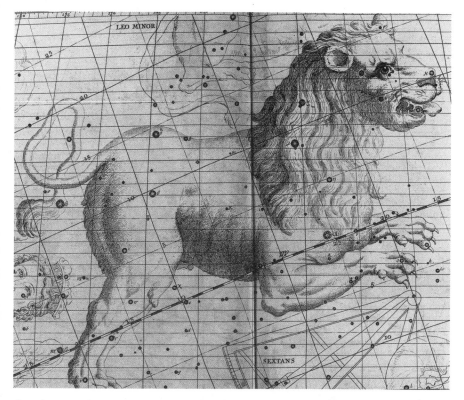

Leo shown ready to pounce in the *Atlas Coelestis* of John Flamsteed. In his chest can be found the bright star Regulus, labelled Alpha. It lies almost on the Sun's path around the sky, the ecliptic, here marked by a dashed line.

Heracles heaved up his club and made after the animal, which retreated into its cave. Heracles blocked up one of the entrances and went in through the other. He grappled with the lion, locking his huge arm around its throat and choking the beast to death. Heracles carried the lion away in triumph on his shoulders. Later he used the creature's own razor-sharp claws to cut off its pelt, which he wore as a cloak. The lion's gaping mouth bobbing above his own head made Heracles look more fearsome than ever.

It is easy to see the shape of a crouching lion in the stars of Leo, its head being outlined by a sickle-shape of stars. Marking the lion's heart (where Ptolemy located it) is the constellation's brightest star, Alpha Leonis, called Regulus, Latin for 'little king'; its Greek name, Basiliscos, had the same meaning. The tail is marked by the star Beta Leonis, called Denebola from the Arabic for 'the lion's tail'. Gamma Leonis is called Algieba, from the Arabic meaning 'the forehead'; this seems puzzling, since according to Ptolemy it lies in the lion's neck, but the Arabs saw here a very much larger lion than the one seen by the Greeks. Gamma Leonis is a celebrated double star, consisting of a pair of yellow giant stars divisible in small telescopes. Delta Leonis is called Zosma from a Greek word meaning 'girdle' or 'loin cloth', mistakenly applied to this star in Renaissance times.

Leo minor
— the little lion —

A lion cub accompanying Leo, introduced by the Polish astronomer Johannes Hevelius in 1687. It lies between Leo and Ursa Major and was formed from faint stars that were not previously part of any constellation. Its brightest stars are of only fourth magnitude and there are no legends associated with it.

Curiously, Leo Minor has no star labelled Alpha, although there is a Beta Leo Minoris. This seems to have been caused by an oversight on the part of the nineteenth-century English astronomer Francis Baily. Hevelius did not label the stars in any of his newly formed constellations, so 150 years later Baily did it for him. Baily assigned the letter Beta to the second-brightest star in Leo Minor, but left the brightest star unlettered by mistake. According to the historian R.H. Allen, Hevelius gave this star the name Praecipua, meaning 'chief', but the title never caught on.

Leo Minor lies immediately above the head of Leo. From the *Uranographia* of Johann Bode.

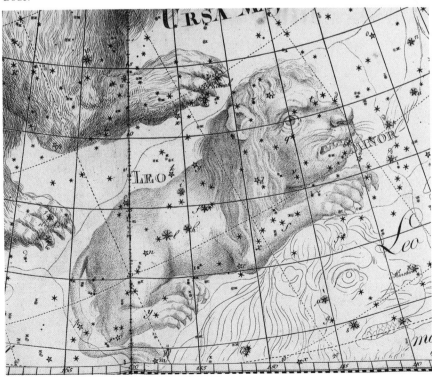

Lepus
— *the hare* —

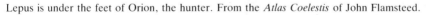

Hermes placed the hare in the sky because of its swiftness, Eratosthenes informs us. Both Eratosthenes and Hyginus referred to the remarkable fertility of hares, as attested to by Aristotle in his *Historia Animalium*: 'Hares breed and bear at all seasons, superfoetate (i.e. conceive again) during pregnancy and bear young every month. They do not give birth to their young all at once, but bring them forth at intervals.'

The celestial hare makes an interesting tableau with Orion and his dogs. Aratus wrote that the Dog (Canis Major) pursues the Hare in an unending race: 'Close behind he rises and as he sets he eyes the setting hare.' But judging by its position in the sky, the hare seems more to be crouched in hiding beneath the hunter's feet.

Hyginus tells us the following moral tale about the hare. At one time there were no hares on the island of Leros, until one man brought in a pregnant female. Soon, everyone began to raise hares and before long the island was swarming with them. They overran the fields and destroyed the crops, reducing the population to starvation. By a concerted effort, the inhabitants drove the hares out of their island. They put the image of the hare among the stars as a reminder that one can easily end up with too much of a good thing.

The constellation's brightest star, third-magnitude Alpha Leporis, is called Arneb, from the Arabic *al-arnab* meaning 'the hare'.

Lepus is under the feet of Orion, the hunter. From the *Atlas Coelestis* of John Flamsteed.

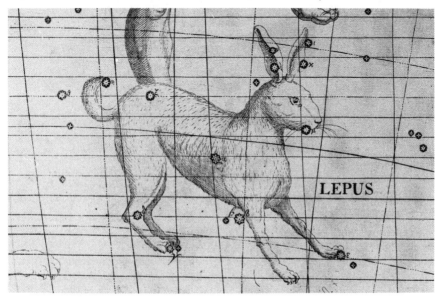

Libra
— *the scales* —

Originally, the area of sky we know as Libra was occupied by the claws of the Scorpion, Scorpius. The Greeks called this area Chelae, literally meaning 'claws', an identification that lives on in the names of the individual stars of Libra (see below). As things have worked out, Libra is now a slightly larger constellation than Scorpius, but it is much less conspicuous.

The identification of this area with a balance became established in the first century BC among the Romans, although exactly when it was introduced and by whom has been lost in the mists of history. To the Romans, Libra was

The balance pans of Libra, depicted in the *Atlas Coelestis* of John Flamsteed.

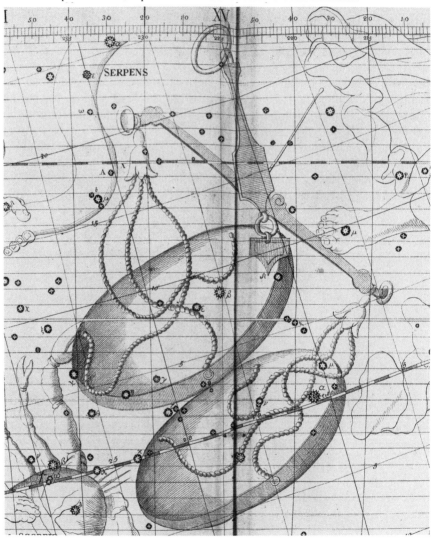

a favoured constellation. The Moon was said to have been in Libra when Rome was founded. 'Italy belongs to the Balance, her rightful sign. Beneath it Rome and her sovereignty of the world were founded', said the Roman writer Manilius. He described Libra as 'the sign in which the seasons are balanced, and the hours of night and day match each other'. This is a hint that the Romans visualized the constellation as a balance because the Sun lay there at the autumn equinox, when day and night are equal. But the idea of a balance in this area did not originate with the Romans, for according to historian Gwyneth Heuter the Sumerians knew this area as ZIB-BA AN-NA, the balance of heaven, 2000 years BC. Hence it seems that the Romans revived a constellation that existed before Greek times.

Libra is the only constellation of the zodiac to represent an inanimate object; the other eleven zodiacal constellations represent animals or people. Once the identification of Libra with a pair of scales became established it was natural to divorce it entirely from Scorpius and to associate it instead with the other neighbouring figure, Virgo, who was identified with Dike or Astraeia, goddess of justice. Libra thus became the scales of justice held aloft by the goddess.

Libra's brightest star, second-magnitude Alpha Librae, is called Zubenelgenubi from the Arabic meaning 'the southern claw', a reminder of the Greek identification of this constellation with the claws of the scorpion. Beta Librae is Zubeneschamali, 'the northern claw'.

Lupus
— *the wolf* —

The ancient Greeks called this constellation Therium, representing an unspecified wild animal, while the Romans called it Bestia, the Beast. It was

Lupus is visualized as being impaled on a pole held by Centaurus. It is shown here in an illustration from the *Uranographia* of Johann Bode.

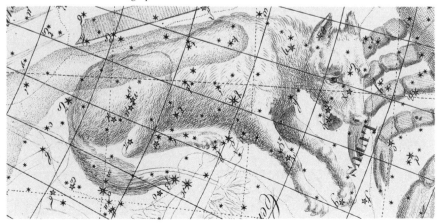

visualized as impaled on a long pole called a *thyrsus*, held by the adjoining constellation of Centaurus, the Centaur. Consequently the constellations of the centaur and the animal were usually regarded as a combined figure.

According to the historian George Michanowsky in his book *The Once and Future Star*, the Babylonians knew this constellation as UR-IDIM, meaning 'wild dog'. Eratosthenes said that the Centaur was holding the animal towards the altar (the constellation Ara) as though about to sacrifice it. Hyginus referred to the animal as simply 'a victim', while Germanicus Caesar said that the centaur was either carrying game from the woods, or was bringing gifts to the altar. The identification of this constellation with a wolf seems to have started in Renaissance times.

One is tempted to recall the story of Lycaon, king of the Arcadians, who served Zeus with the flesh of the god's own son and was punished by being turned into a wolf (see Boötes). But that story has no connection with this constellation, which seems to have been overlooked by the mythologists. The fact that it is an imported constellation probably explains why the Greeks had no myths for it. None of the stars of Lupus have names.

Lynx
— *the lynx* —

Lynx depicted in the *Uranographia* of Johann Bode.

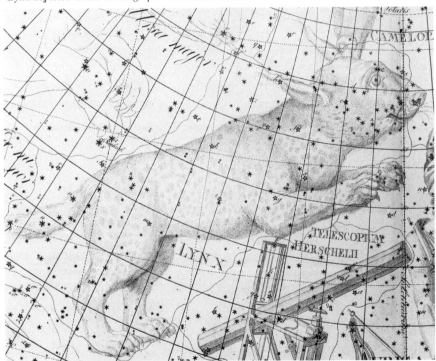

Johannes Hevelius, the Polish astronomer who introduced this constellation in 1687, wrote that one must be as sharp-eyed as a lynx to see its stars, a reference to the fact that he continued to sight star positions with the naked eye long after other astronomers had adopted more accurate telescopic sights. Lynx fills a blank area of sky between Ursa Major and Auriga that is surprisingly large – the constellation covers a greater area of sky than Gemini, for example. Apart from one third-magnitude star, Lynx contains no other stars brighter than fourth magnitude.

It is not known whether Hevelius had in mind the mythological character Lynceus who enjoyed the keenest eyesight in the world – he was even credited with the ability to see things underground. Lynceus and his twin brother Idas sailed with the Argonauts. The pair came to grief when they fell out with those other mythical twins, Castor and Polydeuces (see Gemini).

Lyra
— *the lyre* —

A compact but prominent constellation, marked by the fifth-brightest star in the sky, Vega. Mythologically, Lyra was the lyre of the great musician Orpheus, whose venture into the Underworld is one of the most famous of Greek stories. It was the first lyre ever made, having been invented by Hermes, the son of Zeus and Maia (one of the Pleiades). Hermes made the lyre from the shell of a tortoise that he found browsing outside his cave on Mount Cyllene in Arcadia. Hermes cleaned out the shell, pierced its rim and tied across it seven strings of cow gut, the same as the number of the Pleiades. He also invented the plectrum with which to play the instrument.

The lyre got Hermes out of trouble after a youthful exploit in which he stole some of Apollo's cattle. Apollo angrily came to demand their return, but when he heard the beautiful music of the lyre he let Hermes keep the cattle and took the lyre in exchange. Eratosthenes says that Apollo later gave the lyre to Orpheus to accompany his songs.

Orpheus was the greatest musician of his age, able to charm rocks and streams with the magic of his songs. He was even said to have attracted rows of oak trees down to the coast of Thrace with the music of his lyre. Orpheus joined the expedition of Jason and the Argonauts in search of the golden fleece. When the Argonauts heard the tempting song of the Sirens, sea nymphs who had lured generations of sailors to destruction, Orpheus sang a counter melody that drowned the Sirens' voices.

Later, Orpheus married the nymph Eurydice. One day, Eurydice was spied by Aristaeus, a son of Apollo, who attacked her in a fit of passion. Fleeing from him, she stepped on a snake and died from its poisonous bite. Orpheus was heartbroken; unable to live without his young wife, Orpheus descended into the Underworld to ask for her release. Such a request was

Lyra was frequently visualized as an eagle or vulture as well as lyre; both are shown on this illustration from the *Uranographia* of Johann Bode. Near the tip of the vulture's beak is the bright star Vega, here spelt Wega; Bode also gave it the alternative name Testa in reference to the tortoise shell from which the lyre was supposedly made by Hermes.

unprecedented. But the sound of his music charmed even the heart of Hades, god of the Underworld, who finally agreed to let Eurydice accompany Orpheus back to the land of the living on one solemn condition: Orpheus must not look behind him until the couple were safely back in daylight.

Orpheus readily accepted, and led Eurydice through the dark passage that led to the upper world, strumming his lyre to guide her. It was an unnerving feeling to be followed by a ghost. He could never be quite sure that his beloved was following, but he dared not look back. Eventually, as they approached the surface, his nerve gave out. He turned round to confirm that Eurydice was still there – and at that moment she slipped back into the depths of the Underworld, out of his grasp for ever.

Orpheus was inconsolable. He wandered the countryside plaintively playing his lyre. Many women offered themselves to the great musician in marriage, but he preferred the company of young boys.

There are two accounts of the death of Orpheus. One version, told by Ovid in his *Metamorphoses*, says that the local women, offended at being rejected by Orpheus, ganged up on him as he sat singing one day. They began to throw rocks and spears at him. At first his music charmed the weapons so that they fell harmlessly at his feet, but the women raised such a din that they eventually drowned the magic music so that their missiles found their target.

Eratosthenes, on the other hand, says that Orpheus incurred the wrath of the god Dionysus by not making sacrifices to him. Orpheus regarded Apollo, the Sun god, as the supreme deity and would often sit on the summit of Mount Pangaeum awaiting dawn so that he could be the first to salute the Sun with his melodies. In retribution for this snub, Dionysus sent his manic followers to tear Orpheus limb from limb. Either way, Orpheus finally joined his beloved Eurydice in the Underworld, while the Muses put the lyre among the stars with the approval of Zeus, their father.

Ptolemy knew the constellation's brightest star simply as Lyra. The name we use for this star today, Vega, comes from the Arabic words *al-nasr al-waqi'* that can mean either 'the swooping eagle' or 'vulture', for the Arabs saw an eagle or vulture here. The constellation was often depicted on star maps as a bird positioned behind a lyre, as it is on the illustration here. It seems that the Arabs visualized Vega and its two nearby stars Epsilon and Zeta Lyrae as an eagle with folded wings, swooping down on its prey, whereas in the constellation Aquila the star Altair and its two attendant stars gave the impression of a flying eagle with its wings outstretched (see Aquila).

Beta Lyrae is called Sheliak, a name that comes from the Arabic for 'harp', in reference to the constellation as a whole. Beta Lyrae is a celebrated variable star. Gamma Lyrae is called Sulafat, from the Arabic meaning 'the tortoise', after the animal from whose shell Hermes made the lyre. Between Beta and Gamma Lyrae lies the Ring Nebula, often pictured in astronomy books; this is a shell of gas thrown off by a dying star.

Mensa
— the table mountain —

A small, faint constellation near the south celestial pole, originally called Mons Mensae, commemorating Table Mountain near Cape Town, South Africa, from where the French astronomer Nicolas Louis de Lacaille charted the southern skies in 1751–52. Mensa contains part of the Large Magellanic Cloud, a neighbour galaxy to our Milky Way, which gives Mensa the appearance of being capped by a white cloud, like the real Table Mountain. Its brightest stars are of only fifth magnitude.

Mensa, introduced by Lacaille under the name Mons Mensae, as illustrated in the *Uranographia* of Johann Bode. Nubecula Major is the Large Magellanic Cloud, representing a cloud capping the mountain.

Microscopium
— the microscope —

One of the southern constellations representing scientific instruments that were invented in 1751–52 by the French astronomer Nicolas Louis de Lacaille. Microscopium lies south of the zodiacal constellation Capricornus in an area of sky containing only fifth-magnitude stars. The only remarkable thing about it is that anyone could imagine a separate constellation here.

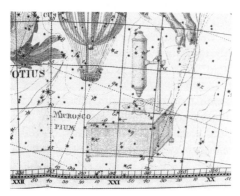

Microscopium shown in the *Uranographia* of Johann Bode.

Monoceros
— *the unicorn* —

The mythological single-horned beast, the unicorn, is represented by this constellation. Monoceros was apparently first depicted in 1613 on a globe attributed to the Dutch theologian and cartographer Petrus Plancius, who gave the constellation its name because a unicorn appears several times in the Old Testament.

Monoceros fills a large area between Hydra and Orion, separating Orion's two dogs. It is not prominent (brightest stars fourth magnitude) but it lies in the Milky Way and contains a host of fascinating objects, most notably the Rosette Nebula, a wreath-shaped mass of glowing gas with embedded stars.

There are no legends associated with Monoceros, and none of its stars are named.

Monoceros, prancing between the two celestial dogs, from the *Atlas Coelestis* of John Flamsteed.

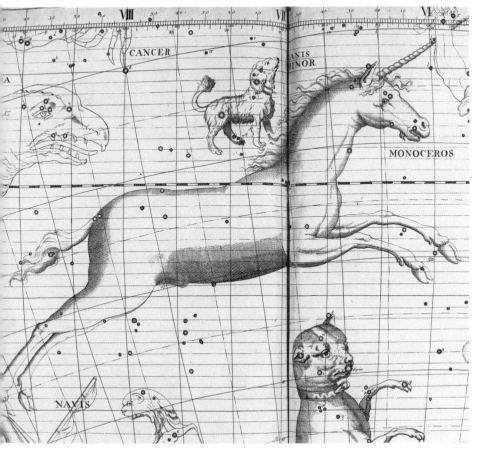

Musca
— the fly —

A small constellation to the south of Crux, the Southern Cross. Musca was originally introduced at the end of the sixteenth century by the Dutch navigators Pieter Dirkszoon Keyser and Frederick de Houtman under the name Apis, the Bee. For a time it was known as Musca Australis, when there was also a northern fly, Musca Borealis, in the sky (see Chapter Four).

The brightest star of Musca is of third magnitude. None of its stars are named, and there are no legends about the fly.

Musca, shown under its earlier name of Apis, in the *Uranographia* of Johann Bode.

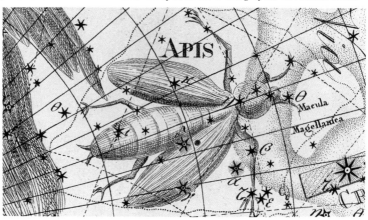

Norma
— the level —

Norma, shown under the name Norma et Regula in the *Uranographia* of Johann Bode.

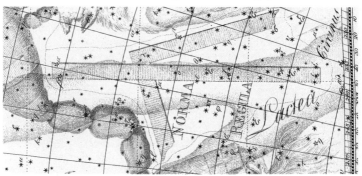

One of the constellations introduced by the French astronomer Nicolas Louis de Lacaille following his mapping of the southern skies in 1751–52. The constellation was often called Norma et Regula on old maps, for it represents a draughtsman's set-square and rule, placed next to the Compasses (Circinus) and a Builder's Level (Triangulum Australe).

The brightest stars of Norma are of only fourth magnitude and none have names. Because of changes in the constellation's boundaries since Lacaille's time, Norma now has no stars labelled Alpha or Beta (the star that Lacaille designated Alpha Normae is now part of Scorpius). Incidentally, Norma shares this distinction with Puppis and Vela, both of which lack stars labelled Alpha and Beta because they were once part of the much larger constellation Argo Navis; when Argo was split into three by Lacaille, the stars Alpha and Beta ended up in the third subdvision, Carina.

Octans
— *the octant* —

Octans represents a navigational instrument, the octant, invented in 1731 by the Englishman John Hadley. It was the forerunner of the modern sextant.

Octans encompasses the south celesital pole, as shown in the *Uranographia* of Johann Bode where it was called Octans Nautica.

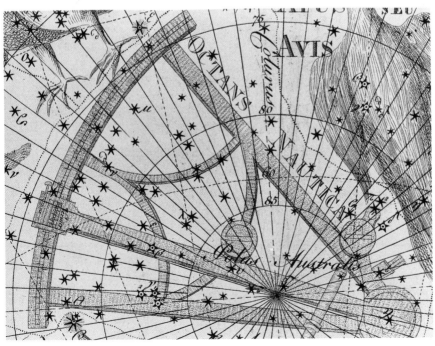

Octans was one of fourteen new figures invented in the 1750s by Nicolas Louis de Lacaille. Fittingly enough for a navigational instrument, Octans encompasses the south celestial pole, but despite this privileged position it contains little of note, consisting of no stars brighter than fourth magnitude.

There is, unfortunately, no southern equivalent of the bright northern pole star, Polaris. The nearest naked-eye star to the south celestial pole is Sigma Octantis, a degree away from the pole, although at magnitude 5.5 it is not prominent.

Ophiuchus
— *the serpent holder* —

Ophiuchus (pronounced off-ee-YOO-cuss) represents a man with a huge snake coiled around his waist. He holds the head of the snake in his left hand and its tail in his right hand. The snake is represented by the constellation Serpens.

The Greeks identified him as Asclepius, the god of medicine. Asclepius was the son of Apollo and Coronis (although some say that his mother was Arsinoe). The story goes that Coronis two-timed Apollo by sleeping with a mortal, Ischys, while she was pregnant by Apollo. A crow brought Apollo

Ophiuchus holds a huge snake, Serpens, in both hands as shown here in the *Atlas Coelestis* of John Flamsteed. Serpens is the only constellation that is divided into two halves.

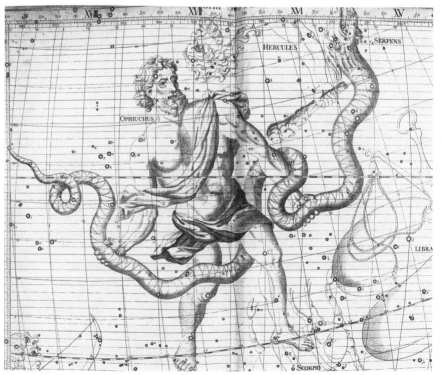

the unwelcome news, but instead of the expected reward the crow, which until then had been snow-white, was cursed by Apollo and turned black.

In a rage of jealousy, Apollo shot Coronis with an arrow. Rather than see his child perish with her, Apollo snatched the unborn baby from its mother's womb as the flames of the funeral pyre engulfed her, and took the infant to Chiron, the wise centaur (represented in the sky by the constellation Centaurus).

Chiron raised Asclepius as his own son, teaching him the arts of healing and hunting. Asclepius became so skilled in medicine that not only could he save lives, he could also raise the dead. On one occasion in Crete, Glaucus, the young son of King Minos, fell into a jar of honey and drowned while at play. As Asclepius contemplated the body of Glaucus, a snake made towards it. He killed the snake with his staff; then another snake came along with a herb in its mouth and placed it on the body of the dead snake, which magically returned to life. Asclepius took the same herb and laid it on the body of Glaucus, whereupon the magical effect was repeated. (Robert Graves suggests that the herb was mistletoe, which the ancients thought had great regenerative properties.) Because of this incident, says Hyginus, Ophiuchus is shown in the sky holding a snake, which became the symbol of healing from the fact that snakes shed their skin every year and are thus seemingly reborn.

Others, though, say that Asclepius received from the goddess Athene the blood of Medusa the Gorgon. The blood that flowed from the veins on her left side was a poison, but the blood from the right side could raise the dead.

Another of the men whom Asclepius supposedly resurrected was Hippolytus, son of Theseus, who died when he was thrown from his chariot (some identify him with the constellation Auriga, the Charioteer). Reaching for his healing herbs, Asclepius touched the boy's chest three times, uttering healing words, and Hippolytus raised his head.

Hades, god of the Underworld, began to realize that the flow of dead souls into his domain would soon dry up if this technique became widely known. He complained to his brother god Zeus who struck down Asclepius with a thunderbolt. Apollo was outraged at this harsh treatment of his son and retaliated by killing the three Cyclopes who forged the thunderbolts of Zeus. To mollify Apollo, Zeus made Asclepius immortal (in the circumstances he could hardly bring him back to life again) and set him among the stars as the constellation Ophiuchus.

The brightest star in Ophiuchus is second-magnitude Alpha Ophiuchi, called Rasalhague from the Arabic meaning 'the head of the serpent collector'. Beta Ophiuchi is called Cebalrai from the Arabic for 'the shepherd's dog'; the Arabs visualized a shepherd (the star Alpha Ophiuchi) along with his dog and some sheep in this area.

Delta and Epsilon Ophiuchi are called Yed Prior and Yed Posterior. These are compound names, formed from the Arabic *al-yad*, meaning 'the hand', with the Latin words *Prior* and *Posterior* added to give names meaning the 'leading' and 'following' part of the hand.

Orion
— *the hunter* —

Orion is the most splendid of constellations, befitting a character who was in legend the tallest and most handsome of men. The constellation is marked out by the brilliant stars Betelgeuse and Rigel, with a distinctive line of three stars forming his belt. 'No other constellation more accurately represents the figure of a man', says Germanicus Caesar.

Manilius calls it 'golden Orion' and 'the mightiest of constellations', and exaggerates its brilliance by saying that, when Orion rises, 'night feigns the brightness of day and folds its dusky wings'. Manilius describes Orion as 'stretching his arms over a vast expanse of sky and rising to the stars with no less huge a stride'. In fact, Orion is not an exceptionally large constellation, ranking only twenty-sixth in size (smaller, for instance, than Perseus according to the modern constellation boundaries), but the brilliance of its stars gives it the illusion of being much larger.

Orion is also one of the most ancient constellations, being among the few star groups known to the earliest Greek writers such as Homer and Hesiod. Even in the space age, Orion remains one of the few star patterns that non-astronomers can recognize.

In the sky, Orion is depicted facing the snorting charge of neighbouring Taurus the Bull, yet the myth of Orion makes no reference to such a combat. However, the constellation originated with the Sumerians, who saw in it their great hero Gilgamesh fighting the Bull of Heaven. The Sumerian name for Orion was URU AN-NA, meaning light of heaven. Taurus was GUD AN-NA, bull of heaven.

Gilgamesh was the Sumerian equivalent of Heracles, which brings us to another puzzle. Being the greatest hero of Greek mythology, Heracles deserves a magnificent constellation such as this one, but in fact is assigned a much more obscure area of sky. So is Orion really Heracles in another guise? It might seem so, for one of the labours of Heracles was to catch the Cretan bull, which would fit the Orion-Taurus conflict in the sky. Ptolemy described him with a club and lion's pelt, both familiar attributes of Heracles, and he is shown this way on old star maps. Despite these facts, no mythologist hints at a connection between this constellation and Heracles.

According to myth, Orion was the son of Poseidon the sea god and Euryale, daughter of King Minos of Crete. Poseidon gave Orion the power to walk on water. Homer in the *Odyssey* describes Orion as a giant hunter, armed with an unbreakable club of solid bronze. In the sky, the hunter's dogs (the constellations Canis Major and Canis Minor) follow at his heels, in pursuit of the hare (the constellation Lepus).

On the island of Chios, Orion wooed Merope, daughter of King Oenopion, apparently without much success, for one night while fortified with wine he tried to ravish her. In punishment, Oenopion put out Orion's eyes and banished him from the island. Orion headed north to the island of

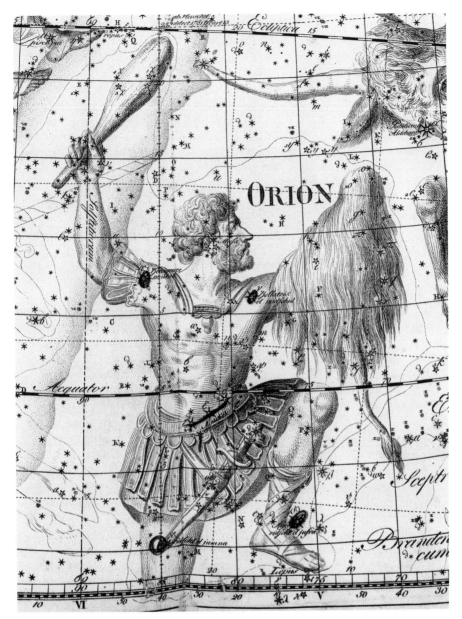

Orion raises his club and shield against the snorting charge of Taurus in this illustration from the *Uranographia* of Johann Bode. His right shoulder is marked by the bright star Betelgeuse, and his left foot by Rigel. A line of three stars forms his belt.

Lemnos where Hephaestus had his forge. Hephaestus took pity on the blind Orion and offered one of his assistants, Cedalion, to act as his eyes. Hoisting the youth on his shoulders, Orion headed east towards the sunrise, which an oracle had told him would restore his sight. As the Sun's healing rays fell on his sightless eyes at dawn, Orion's vision was miraculously restored.

Orion is linked in a stellar myth with the Pleiades star cluster in Taurus. The Pleiades were seven sisters, daughters of Atlas and Pleione. As the story is usually told, Orion fell in love with the Pleiades and pursued them with amorous intent. But according to Hyginus, it was actually their mother Pleione he was after. Zeus snatched the group up and placed them among the stars, where Orion still pursues them across the sky each night.

Stories of the death of Orion are numerous and conflicting. Astronomical mythographers such as Aratus, Eratosthenes and Hyginus were agreed that a scorpion was involved. In one version, told by Eratosthenes and Hyginus, Orion boasted that he was the greatest of hunters. He told Artemis, the goddess of hunting, and Leto, her mother, that he could kill any beast on Earth. The Earth shuddered indignantly and from a crack in the ground came a scorpion which stung the presumptuous giant to death.

Aratus, though, says that Orion attempted to ravish the virgin Artemis, and it was she who caused the Earth to open, bringing forth the scorpion. Ovid has still another account; he says that Orion was killed trying to save Leto from the scorpion. Even the location varies. Eratosthenes and Hyginus say that Orion's death happened in Crete, but Aratus places it in Chios.

In both versions, the outcome was that Orion and the scorpion (the constellation Scorpius) were placed on opposite sides of the sky, so that as Scorpius rises in the east, Orion flees below the western horizon. 'Wretched Orion still fears being wounded by the poisonous sting of the scorpion', noted Germanicus Caesar.

A very different story, also recounted by Hyginus, is that Artemis loved Orion and was seriously considering giving up her vows of chastity to marry him. As the greatest male and female hunters they would have made a formidable couple. But Apollo, twin brother of Artemis, was against the match. One day, while Orion was swimming, Apollo challenged Artemis to demonstrate her skill at archery by hitting a small black object that he pointed out bobbing among the waves. Artemis pierced it with one shot – and was horrified to find that she had killed Orion. Grieving, she placed him among the constellations.

There is a strange and persistent story about the birth of Orion, designed to account for the early version of his name, Urion (even closer to the Sumerian original URU AN-NA). According to this story, there lived in Thebes an old farmer named Hyrieus. One day he offered hospitality to three passing strangers, who happened to be the gods Zeus, Neptune and Hermes. After they had eaten, the visitors asked Hyrieus if he had any wishes. The old man confessed that he would have liked a son, and the three gods promised to fulfil his wish. Standing together around the hide of the ox they had just consumed, the gods urinated on it and told Hyrieus to bury the hide. From it in due course was born a boy whom Hyrieus named Urion after the mode of his conception.

Orion is one of the few constellations in which the star labelled Alpha is not the brightest. The brightest star in Orion is actually Beta Orionis, called Rigel from the Arabic *rijl* meaning 'foot', since Ptolemy described it as marking the left foot of Orion. Rigel is a brilliant blue-white supergiant.

Alpha Orionis is called Betelgeuse (pronounced BET-ell-juice), one of the most famous yet misunderstood star names. It comes from the Arabic *yad al-jauza*, often wrongly translated as 'armpit of the central one'. In fact, it means 'hand of *al-jauza*'. Who (or what) was *al-jauza*? It is the name given by the Arabs to the constellation figure that they saw in this area, seemingly a female figure encompassing the stars of both Orion and Gemini. The word *al-jauza* apparently comes from the Arabic *jwz* meaning middle, so the best translation that modern commentators can offer is that *al-jauza* means something like 'the female one of the middle'. The reference to the 'middle' may be to do with the fact that the constellation lies astride the celestial equator. As Ptolemy described it in the *Almagest*, Betelgeuse represents the right shoulder of Orion. The Greeks did not give a name to either Betelgeuse or Rigel, surprisingly for such prominent stars. Betelgeuse is a red supergiant star, several hundred times the diameter of the Sun, so large that it expands and contracts in size, changing brightness slightly in the process.

The left shoulder of Orion is marked by Gamma Orionis, known as Bellatrix, a Latin name meaning 'the female warrior'. The star at the hunter's right knee, Kappa Orionis, is called Saiph. This name comes from the Arabic for 'sword', and is clearly misplaced. The three stars of the belt – Zeta, Epsilon and Delta Orionis – are called Alnitak, Alnilam and Mintaka. Alnitak and Mintaka both come from the Arabic word meaning 'the belt' or 'girdle'. Alnilam comes from the Arabic meaning 'the string of pearls', another reference to the belt of Orion.

Below the belt lies a hazy patch marking the giant's sword. This is the location of the Orion Nebula, one of the most-photographed objects in the sky, a mass of gas from which a cluster of stars is being born. The gas of the Nebula shines by the light of the stars that have already formed within; it is visible to the naked eye on clear nights.

Pavo
— *the peacock* —

This is one of the twelve constellations introduced into the southern skies at the end of the sixteenth century by the Dutch navigators Pieter Dirkszoon Keyser and Frederick de Houtman. Pavo represents the exotic peacock of India, now a common sight in parks throughout the world. Pavo was first depicted in 1598 on a globe by Petrus Plancius.

In mythology, the peacock was the sacred bird of Hera, who drove through the air in a chariot drawn by peacocks. How the peacock came to have eyes on its tail is the subject of a Greek myth that began one day when Zeus turned his illicit love Io into a white cow to disguise her from his wife,

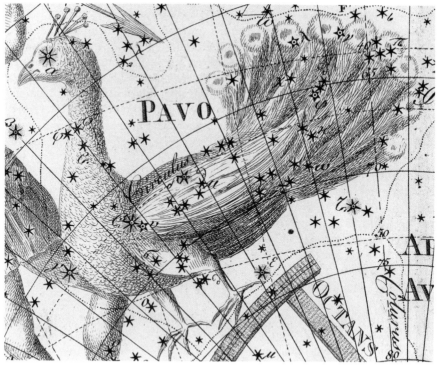

Pavo shown in the *Uranographia* of Johann Bode.

Hera, who nearly caught them together. Hera was suspicious and put the heifer under the guardianship of Argus, who tethered her to an olive tree. Argus was ideally suited for the task of watchman, since he had 100 eyes, of which only two were resting at a time while the others kept watch. Wherever Argus stood, he could always keep several of his eyes on Io.

Zeus sent his son Hermes to release Io from her captivity. Hermes swooped down to Earth and spent the day with Argus, telling him stories and playing his reed pipes until, one by one, the eyes of Argus became sleepy and began to close. When Argus was finally asleep, Hermes lopped off his head and released the heifer. Hera placed the eyes of Argus on the tail of the peacock.

The constellation's brightest star, second-magnitude Alpha Pavonis, is called Peacock.

Pegasus
— *the winged horse* —

Pegasus was the winged horse best known for his association with the Greek hero Bellerophon. The manner of the horse's birth was unusual, to say the least. Its mother was Medusa, the Gorgon, who in her youth was famed for

Only the front half of Pegasus is depicted in the sky, but enough to show his wings. His body is outlined by four stars that form the Square of Pegsus. In front of Pegasus is Equuleus, whose head alone is shown. Illustration from the *Uranographia* of Johann Bode.

her beauty, particularly her flowing hair. Many suitors approached her, but the one who took her virginity was Poseidon, who is both god of the sea and god of horses. Unfortunately, the seduction happened in the temple of Athene. Outraged by having her temple defiled, the goddess Athene changed Medusa into a snake-haired monster whose gaze could turn men to stone.

When Perseus decapitated Medusa, Pegasus and the warrior Chrysaor sprang from her body. The name Pegasus comes from the Greek word *pegai*, meaning 'springs' or 'waters'. Chrysaor's name means 'golden sword', in description of the blade he carried when he was born. Chrysaor played no further part in the story of Pegasus; he later became father of Geryon, the three-bodied monster whom Heracles slew.

Pegasus stretched his wings and flew away from the body of his mother, eventually arriving at Mount Helicon in Boeotia, home of the Muses. There, he struck the ground with his hoof and, to the delight of the Muses, from the rock gushed a spring of water which was named Hippocrene, 'horse's fountain'. The goddess Athene later came to see it.

Pegasus is sometimes depicted as the steed of Perseus, but this is wrong. He was, in fact, ridden by another hero, Bellerophon, son of Glaucus. King Iobates of Lycia sent Bellerophon on a mission to kill the Chimaera, a fire-breathing monster that was devastating Lycia. According to Hesiod the

Chimaera was the offspring of Typhon and Echidne, and had three heads, one like a lion, another like a goat and the third like a dragon. But Homer said in the *Iliad* that it had the front of a lion, the tail of a snake and a middle like a goat, the description that most other authors have followed.

Bellerophon found Pegasus drinking at the spring of Peirene in Corinth and tamed him with a golden bridle given by Athene. Ascending into the sky on the divine horse, Bellerophon swooped down on the Chimaera, killing it with arrows and a lance. After undertaking other tasks for King Iobates, Bellerophon seems to have got over-inflated ideas, for he attempted to fly up on Pegasus to join the gods on Olympus. Before he got there he fell back to Earth; but Pegasus completed the trip and Zeus used him for a while to carry his thunder and lightning, according to Hesiod. Zeus later put Pegasus among the constellations.

Eratosthenes doubted this story because, he said, the horse in the sky has no wings. It is true that Aratus does not mention wings on the celestial horse, but he clearly identifies the constellation as Pegasus, and Ptolemy in his *Almagest* definitely mentions wings, so Eratosthenes must be mistaken. Germanicus Caesar is in no doubt. Pegasus, he writes, 'beats his swift wings in the topmost circle of the sky and rejoices in his stellification'. Eratosthenes repeats the claim of the playwright Euripides that this constellation represents Melanippe, daughter of Chiron the centaur (see Equuleus).

In the sky, only the top half of the horse is shown – even so, it is still the seventh-largest constellation. Its body is represented by the famous Square of Pegasus whose corners are marked by four stars. In Greek times, one star was considered common with Andromeda, marking both the horse's navel and the top of Andromeda's head. Now, it is allocated exclusively to Andromeda, and is known as Alpha Andromedae. The remaining three stars of the Square are Alpha Pegasi, also known as Markab from the Arabic for 'shoulder'; Beta Pegasi, called Scheat from the Arabic meaning 'the shin'; and Gamma Pegasi, or Algenib, meaning 'the side' in Arabic. A star on the horse's muzzle, Epsilon Pegasi, is called Enif from the Arabic meaning 'nose'. Germanicus Caesar said it lies 'where the animal chews the bit, his mouth foaming'.

— *Perseus* —

Perseus is one of the most famous Greek heroes. The characters in the story of Perseus are represented by six constellations that occupy a substantial part of the sky. The constellation depicting Perseus lies in a prominent part of the Milky Way, which is perhaps why Aratus termed him 'dust-stained'.

In Greek myth, Perseus was the son of Danae, daughter of King Acrisius of Argos. Acrisius had locked Danae away in a heavily guarded dungeon when an oracle foretold that he would be killed by his grandson. But Zeus

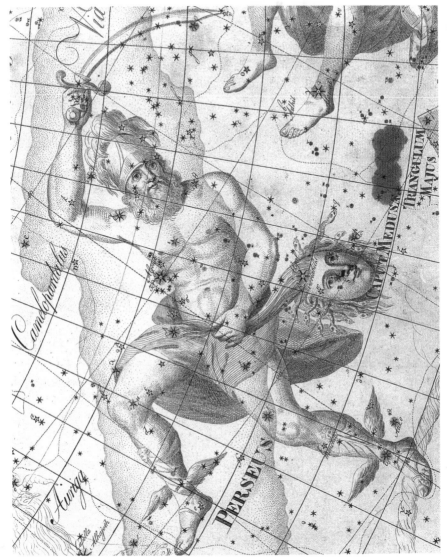

Perseus shown holding the decapitated head of Medusa the Gorgon in the *Uranographia* of Johann Bode. On the forehead of the Gorgon lies the star Algol, famours for its variations in light.

visited Danae in the form of a shower of golden rain that fell through the skylight of the dungeon into her lap and impregnated her. When Acrisius found out, he locked Danae and the infant Perseus into a wooden chest and cast them out to sea.

Inside the bobbing chest Danae clutched her child and prayed to Zeus for deliverance from the sea. A few days later, the chest washed ashore on the island of Seriphos, its cargo still alive but starved and thirsty. A fisherman,

Dictys, broke the chest open and found the mother and child. Dictys brought up Perseus as his own son.

The brother of Dictys was King Polydectes, who coveted Danae as a wife. But Danae was reluctant and Perseus, now grown to manhood, defended her from the king's advances. Instead, King Polydectes hatched a plan to get rid of Perseus. The king pretended that he had turned his attentions instead to Hippodameia, daughter of King Oenomaus of Elis. King Polydectes asked his subjects, including Perseus, to provide horses for a wedding present. Perseus had no horse to give, nor money to buy one, so Polydectes sent him to bring the head of Medusa the Gorgon.

The Gorgons were three hideously ugly sisters called Euryale, Stheno and Medusa. They were the daughters of Phorcys, a god of the sea, and his sister Ceto. The Gorgons had faces covered with dragon scales, tusks like boars, hands of brass and wings of gold. Their evil gaze turned to stone anyone who set eyes on them. Euryale and Stheno were immortal, but Medusa was mortal. She was distinguishable from the others because she had snakes for hair. In her youth Medusa had been famed for her beauty, particularly that of her hair, but she was condemned to a life of ugliness by Athene in whose temple she had been ravished by Poseidon.

A Gorgon's head would be a powerful weapon for a tyrannical king to enforce his rule, but King Polydectes probably thought that Perseus would die in his attempt to obtain it. However, the king had reckoned without Perseus's family connections among the gods. Athene gave him a bronze shield which he carried on his left arm, while in his right hand he wielded a sword of diamond made by Hephaestus. Hermes gave him winged sandals, and on his head he wore a helmet of darkness from Hades that made him invisible.

Under the guidance of Athene, Perseus flew to the slopes of Mount Atlas where the sisters of the Gorgons, called the Graeae, acted as lookouts. The Graeae were poorly qualified for the task, since they had only one eye between the three of them, which they passed to each other in turn. Perseus snatched the eye from them and threw it into Lake Tritonis.

He then followed a trail of statues of men and animals who had been turned to stone by the gaze of the Gorgons. Unseen in his helmet of invisibility, Perseus crept up on the Gorgons and waited until night when Medusa and her snakes were asleep. Looking only at her reflection in his brightly polished shield, Perseus swung his sword and decapitated Medusa with one blow. As Medusa's head rolled to the ground, Perseus was startled to see the winged horse Pegasus and the armed warrior Chrysaor spring fully grown from her body, the legacy of her youthful affair with Poseidon. (Pegasus is commemorated in a constellation of its own.) Perseus rapidly collected up Medusa's head, put it in a pouch and flew away before the other Gorgons awoke.

Drops of blood fell from the head and turned into serpents as they struck the sands of Libya below. Strong winds blew Perseus across the sky like a raincloud, so he stopped to rest in the kingdom of Atlas. When Atlas refused him hospitality, Perseus took out the Gorgon's head and turned him into the range of mountains that now bear his name.

The following morning Perseus resumed his flight, coming to the land of King Cepheus whose daughter Andromeda was being sacrificed to a sea monster. Perseus's rescue of the girl, one of the most famous themes of mythology, is told in detail under the entry for Andromeda. Perseus returned with Andromeda to the island of Seriphos, where he found his mother and Dictys sheltering in a temple from the tyranny of King Polydectes. Perseus stormed into the king's palace to a hostile reception. Reaching into his pouch, Perseus brought out the head of Medusa, turning Polydectes and his followers to stone. Perseus appointed Dictys king of Seriphos. Athene took the head of Medusa and set it in the middle of her shield.

Incidentally, the prophesy that had started all these adventures – namely, that Acrisius would be killed by his grandson – eventually came to pass during an athletic contest when a discus thrown by Perseus accidentally hit Acrisius, one of the spectators, and killed him. Perseus and Andromeda had many children, including Perses, whom they gave to Cepheus to bring up. From Perses, the kings of Persia were said to have been descended.

In the sky, Perseus lies next to his beloved Andromeda. Nearby are her parents Cepheus and Cassiopeia, as well as the monster, Cetus, to which she was sacrificed. Pegasus the winged horse completes the tableau. Perseus himself is shown holding the Gorgon's head. The star that Ptolemy called 'the bright one in the Gorgon head' is Beta Persei, named Algol from the Arabic *ra's al-ghul* meaning 'the demon's head'. Algol is the type of star known as an eclipsing binary, consisting of two close stars that orbit each other, in this case every 2.9 days. Algol varies in brightness as the two stars eclipse each other. Its variability was discovered in 1669 by the Italian astronomer Geminiano Montanari.

The brightest star in the constellation, second-magnitude Alpha Persei, has two alternative names. One is Mirfak, from the Arabic for 'elbow'. The other name is Algenib from the Arabic meaning 'the side', which is where Ptolemy described it as lying. Perseus is depicted holding aloft his sword in his right hand. This hand is marked by what Ptolemy termed a 'nebulous mass' – in fact, a twin cluster of stars now called, appropriately, the Double Cluster.

Phoenix
— *the phoenix* —

A constellation representing the mythical bird that supposedly was reborn from its own ashes. The constellation was invented at the end of the sixteenth century by the Dutch navigators Pieter Dirkszoon Keyser and Frederick de Houtman.

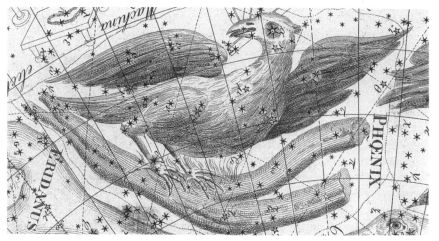

Phoenix emerging from the funeral pyre, as shown in the *Uranographia* of Johann Bode.

Ovid in his *Metamorphoses* tells us that the phoenix lived for 500 years, eating the gum of incense and the sap of balsam. At the end of its alloted span the bird built itself a nest from cinnamon bark and incense among the topmost branches of a palm tree, ending its life on the fragrantly scented nest. A baby phoenix was born from its father's body. The nest was both the tomb of one phoenix and the cradle of the next. When it was old enough to carry the weight, the young phoenix lifted the nest from the tree and carried it to the temple of Hyperion, the Titan who was the father of the Sun god.

Pictor
— *the painter's easel* —

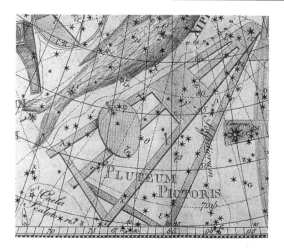

One of the constellations representing technical and artistic apparatus that the Frenchman Nicolas Louis de Lacaille introduced into the southern sky after his observing expedition to the Cape of Good Hope in 1751–52. Lacaille's original title for the constellation was Equuleus Pictoris, which has since been shortened. Bode termed it Pluteum Pictoris. Lacaille visualized the constellation as a painter's easel and palette.

Pisces
— *the fishes* —

The mythological events concerning this constellation are said to have taken place around the Euphrates river, a strong indication that the Greeks inherited this constellation from the Babylonians. The story follows an early episode in Greek mythology, in which the gods of Olympus had defeated the Titans and the Giants in a power struggle. Mother Earth, also known as Gaia, had another nasty surprise in store for the gods. She coupled with Tartarus, the lowest region of the Underworld where Zeus had imprisoned the Titans, and from this unlikely union came Typhon, the most awful monster the world had ever seen.

According to Hesiod, Typhon had a hundred dragon's heads from which black tongues flicked out. Fire blazed from the eyes in each of these heads,

A cord joins the tails of Pisces, the two fishes. From the *Atlas Coelestis* of John Flamsteed.

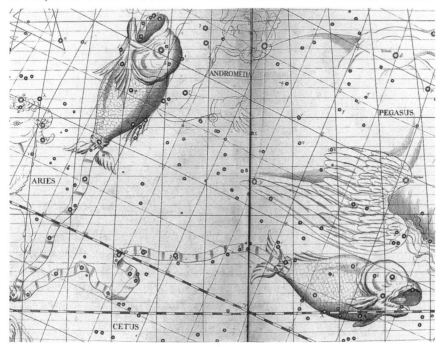

and from them came a cacophony of sound: sometimes ethereal voices which gods could understand, while at other times Typhon bellowed like a bull, roared like a lion, yelped like puppies, or hissed like a nest of snakes.

Gaia sent this fearful monster to attack the gods. Pan saw him coming and alerted the others with a shout. Pan himself jumped into the river and changed his form into a goat-fish, represented by the constellation Capricornus, also inherited from the Babylonians.

Aphrodite and her son Eros took cover among the reeds on the banks of the Euphrates, but when the wind rustled the undergrowth Aphrodite became fearful. Holding Eros in her lap she called for help to the water nymphs and leapt into the river. In one version of the story, two fishes swam up and carried Aphrodite and Eros to safety on their backs, although in another version the two refugees were themselves changed into fish. The mythologists said that because of this story the Syrians would not eat fish. An alternative story, given by Hyginus in the *Fabulae*, is that an egg fell into the Euphrates and was rolled to the shore by some fish. Doves sat on the egg and from it hatched Aphrodite who, in gratitude, put the fish in the sky. Eratosthenes wrote that the fish represented by Pisces were offspring of another fish that is represented by the constellation Piscis Austrinus.

In the sky, the two fish of Pisces are represented swimming in opposite directions, their tails joined by a cord. The Greeks offered no good explanation for this cord, but according to the historian Paul Kunitzsch the Babylonians visualized a pair of fish joined by a cord in this area, so evidently the Greeks borrowed this idea although the significance of the cord was lost.

Pisces is a disappointingly faint constellation, its brightest stars being of only fourth magnitude. Alpha Piscium is called Alrescha, from the Arabic name meaning 'the cord'. It lies where the cords joining the two fish are knotted together. Pisces is notable because it contains the point at which the Sun crosses the celestial equator into the northern hemisphere each year. This point, called the vernal equinox, originally lay in Aries, but it has now moved into Pisces because of a slow wobble of the Earth on its axis called precession.

Piscis austrinus
— *the southern fish* —

Eratosthenes called this the great fish, and said that it was the parent of the two smaller fishes of Pisces. Like Pisces, its mythology has a Middle Eastern setting that reveals its Babylonian origin. According to the brief account of Eratosthenes, the Syrian fertility goddess Derceto (the Greek name for Atargatis) is supposed to have fallen into a lake at Bambyce near the Euphrates river in Syria, and was saved by a large fish. Hyginus says, in repetition of his note on Pisces, that as a result of this the Syrians do not eat

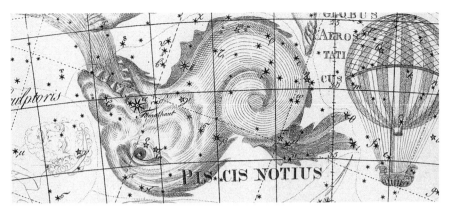

Piscis Austrinus, called Piscis Notius on the *Uranographia* of Johann Bode, is shown drinking water from the urn of Aquarius. In its mouth lies the bright star Fomalhaut.

fish but they worship the images of fish as gods. All the accounts of this constellation's mythology are disappointingly sketchy.

Bambyce later became known to the Greeks as Hieropolis (meaning sacred city), now called Membij. Other classical sources tell us that temples of Atargatis contained fish ponds. The goddess was said to punish those who ate fish by making them ill, but her priests ate fish in a daily ritual.

According to the Greek writer Diodorus Siculus, Derceto deliberately threw herself into a lake at Ascalon in Palestine as a suicide bid in shame for a love affair with a young Syrian, Caystrus, by whom she bore a daughter, Semiramis. Derceto killed her lover and abandoned her child, who was brought up by doves and later became queen of Babylon. In the lake, Derceto was turned into a mermaid, half woman, half fish.

Piscis Austrinus is more noticeable than Pisces in the sky because it contains the first-magnitude star Fomalhaut. This name comes from the Arabic meaning 'fish's mouth', which is where Ptolemy described it. In the sky the fish is shown drinking the water flowing from the jar of Aquarius, a strange thing for a fish to do.

Puppis
— *the stern* —

The largest of the three sections into which the ancient constellation of Argo Navis, the ship of the Argonauts, was divided by Nicolas Louis de Lacaille in his catalogue of the southern stars published in 1763. For the mythology of Argo Navis, and an illustration (see Chapter Four). Puppis represents the stern, or poop, of the ship.

Puppis has no stars labelled Alpha or Beta because, when Argo Navis was divided up by Lacaille, the original Greek-letter designations of the stars in Argo were retained; Alpha and Beta ended up in the subdivision of Carina. The brightest star in Puppis is in fact second-magnitude Zeta Puppis, called Naos from the Greek word for 'ship'.

Pyxis
— *the compass* —

A small southern constellation invented by the Frenchman Nicolas Louis de Lacaille during his survey of the southern skies in 1751–52. Pyxis represents a magnetic compass as used by seamen and is located near the stern of the ship Argo. Its brightest stars are of only fourth magnitude and there are no legends associated with it – indeed, the magnetic compass was completely unknown to the ancient Greeks.

In this same area of sky the German astronomer Johann Bode introduced the constellation Lochium Funis, the Log and Line, now obsolete.

Pyxis shown in the *Uranographia* of Johann Bode. Next to it Bode introduced the now-obsolete constellation of Lochium Funis, the Log and Line.

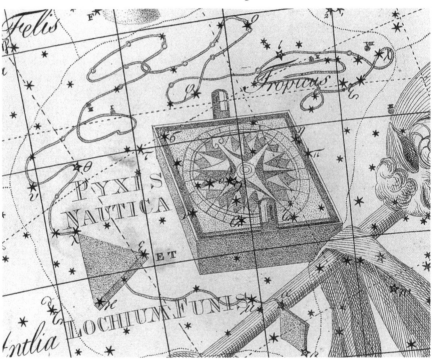

Reticulum
— *the net* —

A small southern constellation, introduced by the French astronomer Nicolas Louis de Lacaille to commemorate the reticle in the eyepiece of his telescope with which he measured star positions from the Cape of Good

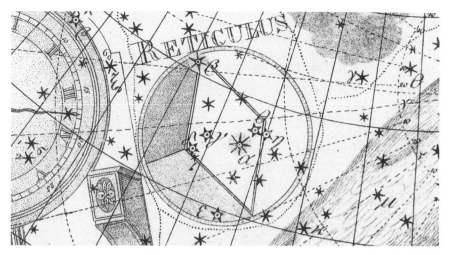

Reticulum, named Reticulus by Johann Bode in his *Uranographia*.

Hope in 1751–52. It replaced a previous constellation called Rhombus introduced in 1621 by the German astronomer Isaac Habrecht. The constellation's brightest star, Alpha Reticuli, is of third magnitude, but is not named.

Sagitta
— *the arrow* —

This is the third-smallest constellation in the sky, with no stars brighter than fourth magnitude, but it was well-known to the Greeks. Aratus described it as 'alone, without a bow' since there is no sign of the archer who might have shot it.

There are at least three different stories to account for the arrow in the sky. Eratosthenes said it was the weapon with which Apollo killed the

Sagitta flying near the feet of Vulpecula, from the *Atlas Coelestis* of John Flamsteed.

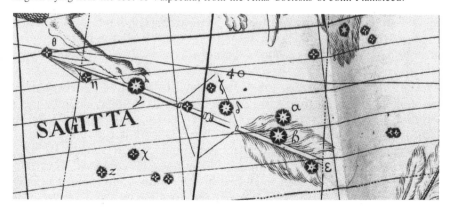

Cyclopes because they made the thunderbolts of Zeus that struck down Apollo's son, Asclepius. According to this story, Asclepius was a great healer with the power to raise the dead, but Zeus killed Asclepius when Hades, god of the Underworld, complained that he was losing business. Asclepius is commemorated in the constellation Ophiuchus.

Hyginus said that Sagitta was one of the arrows with which Heracles killed the eagle that ate the liver of Prometheus. It was Prometheus who moulded men out of clay in the likeness of the gods, and gave them fire that he had stolen from Zeus. Prometheus carried the fire triumphantly in a vegetable stalk like a runner bearing the Olympic torch. Zeus cruelly punished him for this theft by chaining him to Mount Caucasus, where a long-winged eagle ate his liver during the day. But at night the liver grew back again for the eagle to resume his feast in the morning. Heracles freed Prometheus from this torture by shooting the eagle with an arrow.

Germanicus Caesar identified Sagitta as the arrow of Eros which kindled in Zeus his passion for the shepherd boy Ganymede, who is commemorated in the constellation Aquarius. Now, according to Germanicus, the arrow is guarded in the sky by the eagle of Zeus – and Sagitta does indeed lie next to the constellation of the eagle, Aquila.

None of the stars of Sagitta are named.

Sagittarius
— the archer —

Sagittarius is depicted in the sky as a centaur, with the body and four legs of a horse but the upper torso of a man. He is shown wearing a cloak and drawing a bow, aimed in the direction of the neighbouring Scorpion. Aratus spoke of the Bow and the Archer as though they were separate constellations. Sagittarius is sometimes misidentified as Chiron. But Chiron is in fact represented by the other celestial centaur, the constellation Centaurus.

Sagittarius is a constellation of Sumerian origin, subsequently adopted by the Greeks, and this helps explain the confusion surrounding its identity. Eratosthenes doubted that this constellation was a centaur, giving as one of his reasons the fact that centaurs did not use bows. Instead, Eratosthenes described Sagittarius as a two-footed creature with the tail of a satyr. He said that this figure was Crotus, son of Eupheme, the nurse to the Muses, who were nine daughters of Zeus. According to the Roman mythographer Hyginus, the father of Crotus was Pan, which confirms the view of Eratosthenes that he should be depicted as a satyr rather than a centaur.

Crotus invented archery and often went hunting on horseback. He lived on Mount Helicon among the Muses, who enjoyed his company. They sang for him, and he applauded them loudly. The Muses requested that Zeus place him in the sky, where he is seen demonstrating the art of archery. By

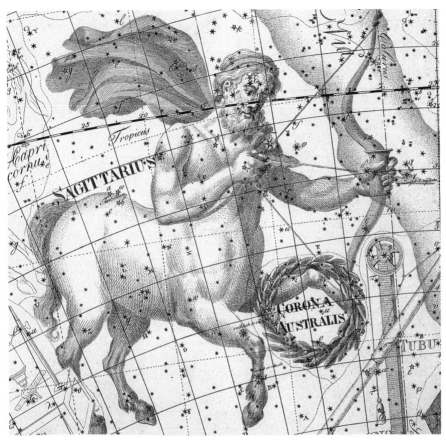

Sagittarius, the centaur-like archer, shown drawing his bow in the *Uranographia* of Johann Bode.

his forefeet is a circle of stars that Hyginus said was a wreath thrown off by someone at play. This circlet of stars is the constellation Corona Australis.

Alpha Sagittarii is alternatively called Rukbat or Alrami, both from the Arabic *rukbat al-rami*, 'knee of the archer'. Beta Sagittarii is called Arkab, from the Arabic name meaning 'the archer's Achilles tendon'. Gamma Sagittarii is Alnasl, fom the Arabic meaning 'the point', referring to the archer's arrow.

Delta, Epsilon and Lambda Sagittarii are respectively called Kaus Media, Kaus Australis and Kaus Borealis. The word Kaus comes from the Arabic *al-qaus*, 'the bow', and the suffixes are Latin words signifying the middle, southern and northern parts of the bow. Zeta Sagittarii is Ascella, a Latin word meaning 'armpit'. All these names closely follow the descriptions of the stars' positions given by Ptolemy in his Almagest.

Last, but not least, is Sigma Sagittarii, called Nunki. This name was applied relatively recently by navigators, but it was borrowed from a list of Babylonian star names. The Babylonian name NUN-KI was given to a group of stars representing their sacred city of Eridu on the Euphrates. The name has now been applied exclusively to Sigma Sagittarii, and is said to be the oldest star name in use.

Sagittarius contains a rich part of the Milky Way, lying towards the centre of our Galaxy. The exact centre of the Galaxy is believed to be marked by a radio-emitting source that astronomers call Sagittarius A. There are many notable objects in Sagittarius, including the Lagoon Nebula and the Trifid Nebula, two clouds of gas lit up by stars inside them.

Scorpius
— *the scorpion* —

'There is a certain place where the scorpion with his tail and curving claws sprawls across two signs of the zodiac', said Ovid in his *Metamorphoses*. He was referring to the ancient Greek version of Scorpius, which was much larger than the constellation we know today. The Greek scorpion was in two halves: one half contained his body and its sting, while the front half comprised the claws. The Greeks called this front half Chelae, meaning 'claws'. In the first century BC the Romans made the claws into a separate constellation, Libra, the Balance.

In mythology, this is the scorpion that stung Orion the hunter to death, although accounts differ as to the exact circumstances. Eratosthenes offers two versions. Under his description of Scorpius he says that Orion tried to ravish Artemis, the hunting goddess, and that she sent the scorpion to sting him, an account that is supported by Aratus. But in his entry on Orion, Eratosthenes says that the Earth sent the scorpion to sting Orion after he had boasted that he could kill any wild beast. Hyginus also gives both stories. Aratus says that the death of Orion happened on the island of Chios, but Eratosthenes and Hyginus place it in Crete.

In either case, the moral is that Orion suffers retribution for his hubris. This seems to be one of the oldest of Greek myths the origin of which may lie in the sky itself, since the two constellations are placed opposite each other so that Orion sets as his conqueror the scorpion rises. But the constellation is much older than the Greeks, for the Sumerians knew it as GIR-TAB, the Scorpion, over 5000 years ago.

Scorpius clearly resembles a scorpion, particularly the curving line of stars that form its tail with its sting raised to strike. Old star maps show one foot of Ophiuchus awkwardly overlapping the scorpion's body. Incidentally, Scorpius is the modern astronomical name for the constellation; Scorpio is the old name, used by astrologers.

The brightest star in Scorpius is the brilliant Antares, a name that comes from the Greek meaning 'like Mars' (often translated as 'rival of Mars') on account of its strong reddish-orange colour, similar to that of the planet Mars. Antares is a remarkable supergiant star, several hundred times the

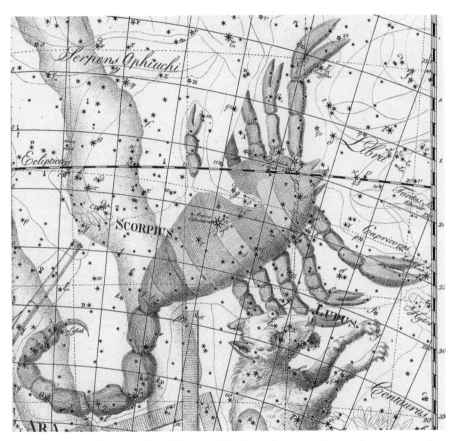

Scorpius from the *Uranographia* of Johann Bode. Part of the scorpion's body is overlapped by the foot of Ophiuchus. In the middle of the scorpion's body lies the red star Antares. On this chart, Bode also names it Calbalacrab, from the Arabic meaning 'scorpion's heart'.

size of our Sun. Beta Scorpii is called Graffias, Latin for 'claws'. This star is sometimes also known as Acrab, from the Arabic for 'scorpion'. Delta Scorpii is called Dschubba, a strange name that is a corruption of the Arabic word meaning 'forehead', in reference to its position in the middle of the scorpion's head. At the end of the scorpion's tail lies Lambda Scorpii, called Shaula from the Arabic meaning 'the sting'.

Sculptor
— *the sculptor* —

A faint constellation south of Cetus and Aquarius, invented by the French astronomer Nicolas Louis de Lacaille during his mapping of the southern skies in 1751–52. Its original name was Apparatus Sculptoris, since shortened. Sculptor represents a sculptor's studio, complete with a fine marble head on a platform and a mallet and chisel. The stars of Sculptor are of fourth magnitude and fainter, and none are named.

Apparatus Sculptoris was the name under which Lacaille introduced the constellation known today as Sculptor. From the *Uranographia* of Johann Bode.

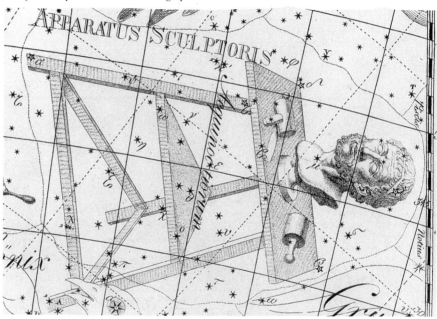

Scutum
— *the shield* —

The fifth-smallest constellation in the sky, introduced by the Polish astronomer Johannes Hevelius in 1684 under the title Scutum Sobiescianum, Sobiesci's Shield, in honour of King John III Sobiesci of Poland. It is the only constellation introduced for political reasons that is still in use.

Scutum lies in a bright area of the Milky Way and is distinctive despite its small size. The brightest stars of Scutum are of only fourth magnitude, and none are named, but the constellation contains a celebrated cluster of stars called the Wild Duck cluster because its fan-shape resembles a flight of ducks.

Scutum as it was shown on the *Uranographia* of Johann Bode.

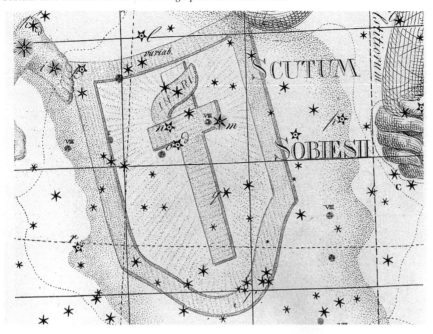

Serpens
— *the serpent* —

This constellation is unique, for it is divided into two parts – Serpens Caput, the head, and Serpens Cauda, the tail. But astronomers regard it as a single constellation. Serpens represents a huge snake held by the constellation Ophiuchus. In his left hand Ophiuchus grasps the snake's head, which is turned to look back at him, while his right hand holds the tail. Aratus and Manilius agreed that Serpens was coiled around the body of Ophiuchus, but most star atlases show the snake simply passing between his legs.

In mythology, Ophiuchus was identified as the healer Asclepius, son of Apollo, although why he appears to be wrestling with a serpent in the sky is not fully explained. His connection with snakes is attributed to the story that he once killed a snake that was miraculously restored to life by a herb placed on it by another snake. Asclepius subsequently used the same technique to revive dead people. Snakes are the symbol of rebirth because they shed their skins every year.

The star Alpha Serpentis is called Unukalhai from the Arabic meaning 'the serpent's neck', where it is located. The tip of the serpent's tail is marked by Theta Serpentis, called Alya, an Arabic word that actually refers to 'a sheep's tail'. The most celebrated object in Serpens is a star cluster called M16, embedded in a gas cloud called the Eagle Nebula.

Sextans
— the sextant —

A faint constellation south of Leo, introduced by the Polish astronomer Johannes Hevelius in 1687 under the name Sextans Uraniae to commemorate the instrument with which he measured star positions. Hevelius continued to make naked-eye sightings with his sextant throughout his life, even though telescopes were available; it was perhaps to demonstrate the keenness of his eyes that he formed Sextans out of such faint stars, as he did with another of his inventions, Lynx. The brightest star in Sextans is of magnitude 4.5 and none of the stars is named.

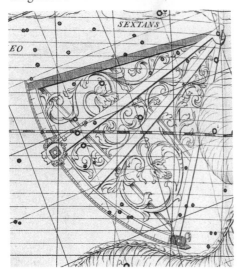

Sextans illustrated in the *Atlas Coelestis* of John Flamsteed.

Taurus
— the bull —

Taurus is a distinctive constellation, with a head defined by a V-shaped group of stars and star-tipped horns. Two Greek bull-myths were associated with Taurus. Usually it was said to represent Zeus in the disguise he adopted for another of his extramarital affairs, this time as the bull that carried away Europa, daughter of King Agenor of Phoenicia.

Europa liked to play on the beach with the other girls of Tyre. Zeus instructed his son Hermes to drive the king's cattle from their pastures on the mountain slopes towards the shore where the girls were playing. Adopting the shape of a bull, Zeus surreptitiously mingled with the lowing herd, awaiting his chance to abduct Europa. There was no mistaking who was the most handsome bull. His hide was white as fresh snow and his horns shone like polished metal.

Europa was entranced by this beautiful yet placid creature. She adorned his horns with flowers and stroked his flanks, admiring the muscles on his neck and the folds of skin on his flanks. The bull kissed her hands, while inwardly Zeus could hardly contain himself in anticipation of the final

Taurus charges head down towards Orion, as depicted in the *Atlas Coelestis* of John Flamsteed. Only the front part of Taurus is shown in the sky. The bull's eye is marked by the reddish star Aldebaran, and on his back is the Pleiades star cluster. One horn ends at the foot of Auriga.

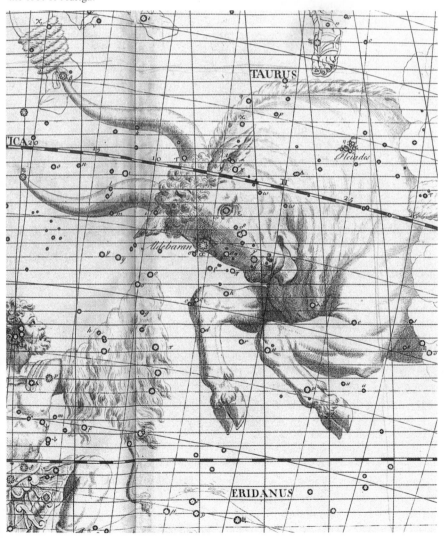

conquest. The bull lay on the golden sands and Europa ventured to sit on his back. At first, she feared nothing when the bull rose and began to paddle in the surf. But she became alarmed when it began to swim strongly out to sea. Europa looked around in dismay at the receding shoreline and clung tightly to the bull's horns as waves washed over the bull's back. Craftily, Zeus the bull dipped more deeply into the water to make her hold him more tightly still.

By now, Europa had realized that this was no ordinary bull. Eventually, the bull waded ashore at Crete, where Zeus revealed his true identity and seduced Europa. He gave her presents that included a dog that later became the constellation Canis Major. The offspring of Zeus and Europa included Minos, king of Crete, who established the famous palace at Knossos where bull games were held.

An alternative story says that Taurus may represent Io, another illicit love of Zeus, whom the god turned into a heifer to disguise her from his wife Hera. But Hera was suspicious and set the hundred-eyed watchman Argus to guard the heifer. At the request of Zeus, Hermes killed Argus and freed the heifer. Hera, furious at this, sent a gadfly to chase the heifer, who threw herself into the sea and swam away.

In the sky, only the front half of the bull is shown. This can be explained mythologically by assuming that the rear quarters are submerged. In reality, there is no space in the sky to show the complete bull, for the constellations Cetus and Aries lie where the bull's rear quarters should be. Taurus shares with Pegasus this uncomfortable fate of having been cut in half in the sky.

Taurus is depicted on star maps as sinking on one leg, perhaps to entice Europa onto its back. Manilius described the bull as lame and drew a moral from it: 'The sky teaches us to undergo loss with fortitude, since even constellations are fashioned with limbs deformed', he wrote.

The face of Taurus is marked by the V-shaped group of stars called the Hyades. Ovid in his *Fasti* asserts that the name comes from the old Greek word *hyein*, meaning 'to rain', so that Hyades means 'rainy ones', because their rising at certain times of year was said to be a sign of rain. In mythology the Hyades were the daughters of Atlas and Aethra the oceanid. Their eldest brother was Hyas, a bold hunter who one day was killed by a lioness. His sisters wept inconsolably – Hyginus says they died of grief – and for this they were placed in the sky. Hence it seems equally likely that their name comes from their brother Hyas. In another story, the Hyades were nymphs who nursed the infant Dionysus in their cave on Mount Nysa, feeding him on milk and honey. The Romans had a different name; they called the Hyades *suculae* meaning 'piglets'.

The mythographers were massively confused about the names and even the number of the Hyades. They are variously described as being five or seven in number. The Greek astronomer Ptolemy listed five Hyades in his star catalogue. Hyginus alone gives four different lists of their names, none of which agrees completely with the list of five originally given by Hesiod, viz: Phaesyle, Coronis, Cleia, Phaeo and Eudore. Astronomers have avoided the problem by not naming any of the stars of the Hyades.

Binoculars and small telescopes show many more members of the Hyades than are visible to the naked eye. In all, several hundred stars belong to the cluster, which lies 150 light years away.

Even more famous than the Hyades is another star cluster in Taurus: the Pleiades, commonly known as the Seven Sisters. To the eye, the Pleiades cluster appears as a fuzzy patch like a swarm of flies over the back of the bull. According to Hyginus, some ancient astronomers called them the bull's tail. So distinctive are the Pleiades that the ancient Greeks regarded them as a separate mini-constellation and used them as a calendar marker. Hesiod, in his agricultural poem *Works and Days*, instructs farmers to begin harvesting when the Pleiades rise at dawn, which in Greek times would have been in May, and to plough when they set at dawn, which would have been in November. Ptolemy did not list individual members of the Pleiades in his *Almagest*, giving only an indication of the cluster's extent.

In mythology the Pleiades were the seven daughters of Atlas and the oceanid Pleione, after whom they are named. One popular derivation is that the name comes from the Greek word *plein*, meaning 'to sail' – so Pleione means 'sailing queen' and the Pleiades are the 'sailing ones', because in Greek times they were visible all night during the summer sailing season. When the Pleiades vanished from the night sky, it was considered prudent to stay ashore. 'Gales of all winds rage when the Pleiades, pursued by violent Orion, plunge into the clouded sea', wrote Hesiod.

Alternatively, and possibly more likely, the name may come from the old Greek word *pleos*, 'full', which in the plural meant 'many', a suitable reference to the cluster. According to other authorities, the name comes from the Greek word *peleiades*, meaning 'flock of doves'.

Unlike their half-sisters the Hyades, the names of all seven Pleiades are assigned to stars in the cluster: Alcyone, Asterope (also known as Sterope), Celaeno, Electra, Maia, Merope and Taygete. Two more stars are named after their parents, Atlas and Pleione. Alcyone is the brightest star in the cluster. According to mythology, Alcyone and Celaeno were both seduced by Poseidon. Maia, the eldest and most beautiful of the sisters, was seduced by Zeus and gave birth to Hermes; she later became foster-mother to Arcas, son of Zeus and Callisto. Zeus also seduced two other Pleiades: Electra, who gave birth to Dardanus, the founder of Troy; and Taygete, who gave birth to Lacedaemon, founder of Sparta. Asterope was ravished by Ares and became mother of Oenomaus, king of Pisa. Hence six Pleiades became paramours of the gods. Only Merope married a mortal, Sisyphus, a notorious trickster who was subsequently condemned to roll a stone eternally up a hill.

Although the Pleiades are popularly termed 'the Seven Sisters', only six stars are easily visible to the naked eye, and a considerable mythology has grown up to account for the 'missing' Pleiad. Eratosthenes says that Merope was the faint Pleiad because she was the only one who married a mortal. Hyginus and Ovid also recount this story, giving her shame as the reason for her faintness, but both add another candidate: Electra, who could not bear to see the fall of Troy, which had been founded by her son Dardanus. Hyginus says that, moved by grief, she left the Pleiades altogether, but Ovid says that she merely covered her eyes with her hand. Astronomers, however, have not followed either legend in their naming of the stars, for the faintest named Pleiad is actually Asterope.

Binoculars show dozens of stars in the Pleiades, and in all the cluster contains several hundred stars. The Pleiades lie 400 light years away, nearly three times farther than the Hyades. They are relatively young by stellar standards, the youngest being no more than a few million years old. Long-exposure photographs show that the Pleiades are still enveloped in traces of the cloud from which they formed.

A famous myth links the Pleiades with Orion. As Hyginus tells it, Pleione and her daughters were one day walking through Boeotia when Orion tried to ravish her. Pleione and the girls escaped, but Orion pursued them for seven years. Zeus immortalized the chase by placing the Pleiades in the heavens where Orion follows them endlessly.

The bull's glinting red eye is marked by the brightest star in Taurus, Aldebaran, a name that comes from the Arabic meaning 'the follower', referring to the fact that it follows the Pleiades across the sky. Surprisingly for such a prominent star, Greek astronomers had no name for it (although Ptolemy called it Torch in his *Tetrabiblos*, a book about astrology). Aldebaran appears to lie among the Hyades but in fact it is a foreground object about halfway between us and the cluster, and so is superimposed on the Hyades by chance. Aldebaran is a red giant star about forty times the diameter of the Sun.

Marking the left horn of the bull is the star Elnath, a name that comes from the Arabic meaning 'the butting one'. Ptolemy described this star as being common with the right foot of Auriga, the Charioteer, but now it is the exclusive property of Taurus.

Near the tip of the bull's right horn, the star Zeta Tauri, lies the remarkable Crab Nebula, the result of one of the most celebrated events in the history of astronomy – a stellar explosion, seen from Earth in AD 1054, that was bright enough to be visible in daylight for three weeks. We now know that this event was a supernova, the violent death of a massive star, and the Crab Nebula is the shattered remnant of the star that blew up. The Irish astronomer Lord Rosse gave the nebula its name in 1844 because he thought its shape resembled a crab when seen through his telescope. The Crab Nebula lies 6000 light years away, and appears as a misty patch in moderate-sized telescopes.

Telescopium
— *the telescope* —

One of the faint and obscure constellations of the southern sky introduced by the Frenchman Nicolas Louis de Lacaille after his sky-mapping trip to the Cape of Good Hope in 1751–52. It represents one of the long, unwieldy refractors suspended from poles, known as aerial telescopes, used by J.D. Cassini at Paris Observatory. Lacaille originally depicted it as extending between Sagittarius and Scorpius, as shown on the accompanying map by Bode, but modern astronomers have cut off the top of the telescope's tube and its mounting so that it is now restricted to the south of Sagittarius and Corona Australis. Telescopium contains no stars brighter than fourth magnitude.

Telescopium shown under the name Tubus Astronomicus in the *Uranographia* of Johann Bode.

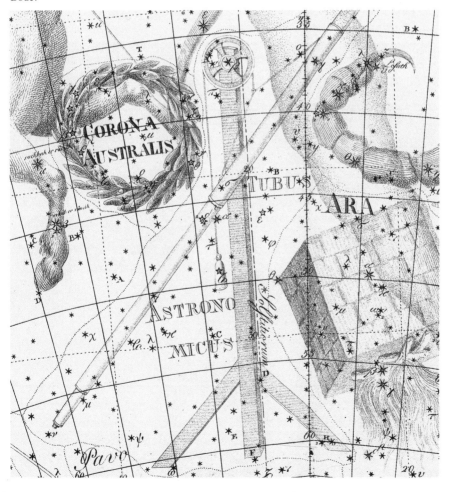

Triangulum
— the triangle —

Since any three points make up the corners of a triangle it is unsurprising, if somewhat unimaginative, to find a triangle among the constellations. Triangulum was known to the Greeks who called it Deltoton, for its shape resembled a capital delta. Aratus described it as an isosceles triangle, having two equal sides and a shorter third side. Eratosthenes said that it represented the Nile river delta. According to Hyginus, some people also saw it as the island of Sicily, which was originally known as Trinacria because of its three promontories. Trinacria was the home of Ceres, goddess of agriculture. Triangulum contains M33, a galaxy in our Local Group, visible in binoculars.

A smaller triangle, Triangulum Minor, was introduced in 1687 by the Polish astronomer Johannes Hevelius from three stars next to Triangulum. Triangulum Minor was shown on some maps, such as the one reproduced here, but has since fallen into disuse.

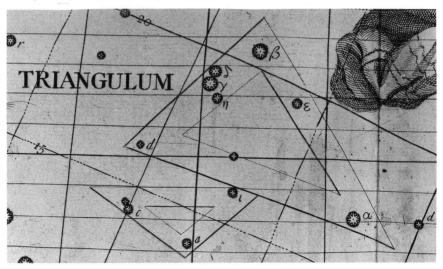

Triangulum from the *Atlas Coelestis* of John Flamsteed. Next to it lies a smaller triangle, once known as Triangulum Minor but now obsolete.

Triangulum australe
— the southern triangle —

The Southern Triangle was among the constellations introduced at the end of the sixteenth century by the Dutch navigators Pieter Dirkszoon Keyser and Frederick de Houtman. A southern triangle was shown on a globe of

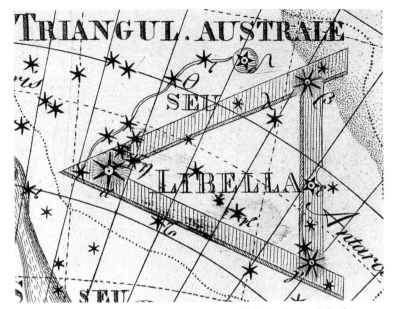

Traingulum Australe, also given the alternative name of Libella the level, in the *Uranographia* of Johann Bode.

1589 by the Dutchman Petrus Plancius, along with a southern cross, but they were not the constellations we know today. The three main stars of Triangulum Australe are brighter than those of their northern counterpart. Navigators have named its brightest star Atria, a contraction of its scientific name Alpha Trianguli Australis.

Tucana
— *the toucan* —

Tucana from the *Uranographia* of Johann Bode. Behind its tail lies Nubecula Minor, the Small Magellanic Cloud, now part of the constellation.

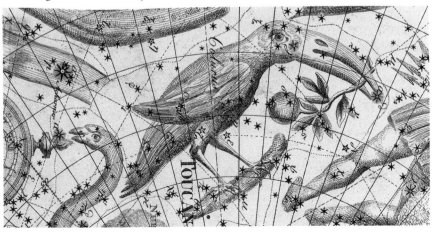

One of the southern constellations devised by the Dutch navigators Pieter Dirkszoon Keyser and Frederick de Houtman at the end of the sixteenth century. It represents the South American bird with a huge bill. Tucana was first depicted in 1598 on a globe by the Dutchman Petrus Plancius. Its brightest star is only of third magnitude, but the constellation is distinguished by two features, firstly the globular star cluster 47 Tucanae, rated the second-best such object in the entire sky, and the Small Magellanic Cloud, the smaller and fainter of the two companion galaxies of our Milky Way. None of the stars of Tucana are named, and there are no legends associated with it.

Ursa major
— *the great bear* —

Undoubtedly the most familiar star pattern in the entire sky is the seven stars that make up the shape popularly termed the Plough or Big Dipper, part of the constellation Ursa Major, the Great Bear. The seven stars form the rump and tail of the bear; the rest of the animal is comprised of fainter stars. It is the third-largest constellation.

In mythology, the Great Bear is identified with two separate characters: Callisto, a paramour of Zeus; and Adrasteia, one of the ash-tree nymphs who nursed the infant Zeus. To complicate matters, there are several different versions of each story, particularly the one involving Callisto.

Callisto is usually said to have been the daughter of Lycaon, King of Arcadia in the central Peloponnese. (An alternative story says that she is not Lycaon's daughter but the daughter of Lycaon's son Ceteus. In this version, Ceteus is identified with the constellation Hercules, kneeling and holding up his hands in supplication to the gods at his daughter's transformation into a bear.)

Callisto joined the retinue of Artemis, goddess of hunting. She dressed in the same way as Artemis, tying her hair with a white ribbon and pinning together her tunic with a brooch, and she soon became the favourite hunting partner of Artemis, to whom she swore a vow of chastity. One afternoon, as Callisto lay down her bow and rested in a shady forest grove, Zeus caught sight of her and was entranced. What happened next is described fully by Ovid in Book II of his *Metamorphoses*. Zeus cunningly assumed the appearance of Artemis and entered the grove to be greeted warmly by the unsuspecting Callisto. He lay beside her and embraced her. Before the startled girl could react, Zeus revealed his true self and, despite Callisto's struggles, had his way with her. Zeus returned to Olympus, leaving the shame-filled Callisto scarcely able to face Artemis and the other nymphs.

On a hot afternoon some months later, the hunting party came to a cool river and decided to bathe. Artemis stripped off and led them in, but

Ursa Major as depicted on the *Uranographia* of Johann Bode. The familiar shape popularly known as the Plough or Big Dipper is made up of seven stars in the rump and tail of the bear.

Callisto hung back. As she reluctantly undressed, her advancing pregnancy was finally revealed. Artemis, scandalized, banished Callisto from her sight.

Worse was to come when Callisto gave birth to a son, Arcas. Hera, the wife of Zeus, had not been slow to realize her husband's infidelity and was now determined to take revenge on her rival. Hurling insults, Hera grabbed Callisto by her hair and pulled her to the ground. As Callisto lay spreadeagled, dark hairs began to sprout from her arms and legs, her hands and feet turned into claws and her beautiful mouth which Zeus had kissed turned into gaping jaws that uttered growls.

For fifteen years Callisto roamed the woods in the shape of a bear, but still with a human mind. Once a huntress herself, she was now pursued by hunters. One day she came face to face with her son Arcas. Callisto recognized Arcas and tried to approach him, but he backed off in fear. He would have speared the bear, not knowing it was really his mother, had not Zeus intervened by sending a whirlwind that carried them up into heaven, where Zeus turned Callisto into the constellation of Ursa Major and Arcas into Boötes.

Hera was now even more enraged to find her rival glorified among the stars, so she consulted her foster parents Tethys and Oceanus, gods of the sea, and persuaded them never to let the bear bathe in the northern waters. Hence, as seen from mid-northern latitudes, the bear never sets below the horizon.

That this is the most familiar version of the myth is due to Ovid's pre-eminence as a story teller, but there are other versions, some older than Ovid. Eratosthenes, for instance, says that Callisto was changed into a bear not by Hera but by Artemis as a punishment for breaking her vow of chastity. Later, Callisto the bear and her son Arcas were captured in the woods by shepherds who took them as a gift to King Lycaon. Callisto and Arcas sought refuge in the temple of Zeus, unaware that Arcadian law laid down the death penalty for trespassers. (Yet another variant says that Arcas chased the bear into the temple while hunting – see Boötes.) To save them, Zeus snatched them up and placed them in the sky.

The Greek mythographer Apollodorus says that Callisto was turned into a bear by Zeus to disguise her from his wife Hera. But Hera saw through the ruse and pointed out the bear to Artemis who shot her down, thinking that she was a wild animal. Zeus sorrowfully placed the image of the bear in the sky.

Aratus makes a completely different identification of Ursa Major. He says that the bear represents one of the nymphs who raised Zeus in the cave of Dicte on Crete. That cave, incidentally, is a real place where local people still proudly point out the place of Zeus's birth. Rhea, his mother, had smuggled Zeus to Crete to escape Cronus, his father. Cronus had swallowed all his previous children at birth for fear that one day they would overthrow him – as Zeus eventually did. Apollodorus names the nurses of Zeus as Adrasteia and Ida, although other sources give different names. Ida is represented by the neighbouring constellation of Ursa Minor, the Little Bear.

These nymphs looked after Zeus for a year, while armed Cretan warriors called the Curetes guarded the cave, clashing their spears against their shields to drown the baby's cries from the ears of Cronus. Adrasteia laid the infant Zeus in a cradle of gold and made for him a golden ball that left a fiery trail like a meteor when thrown into the air. Zeus drank the milk of the she-goat Amaltheia with his foster-brother Pan. Zeus later placed Amaltheia in the sky as the star Capella, while Adrasteia became the Great Bear – although why Zeus turned her into a bear is not explained.

Aratus named the constellation Helice, meaning 'twister', apparently from its circling of the pole, and said that the ancient Greeks steered their ships by reference to it, whereas the Phoenicians used the Little Bear (see Ursa Minor). Aratus said that the bears were also called wagons or wains, from the fact that they wheel around the pole. The adjacent constellation Boötes is visualized as either the herdsman of the bear or the wagon driver. But Germanicus Caesar said that the bears were also called ploughs, because 'the shape of a plough is the closest to the real shape formed by their stars'. According to Hyginus the Romans referred to the Great Bear as

Septentrio, meaning 'seven plough oxen', although he added the information that in ancient times only two of the stars were considered oxen, the other five forming a wagon. On a star map of 1524 the German astronomer Peter Apian showed Ursa Major as a team of three horses pulling a four-wheeled cart, which he called Plaustrum.

One puzzle, never explained by the mythologists, is why the celestial bears have long tails, which real bears do not. Thomas Hood, an English astronomical writer of the late sixteenth century, offered the tongue-in-cheek suggestion that the tails had become stretched when Zeus pulled the bears up into heaven. 'Other reason know I none', he added apologetically.

Two stars in Ursa Major called Dubhe and Merak are popularly termed the Pointers because a line drawn through them points to the north celestial pole. Dubhe's name comes from the Arabic *al-dubb*, 'the bear', while Merak comes from the Arabic word *al-maraqq* meaning 'the flank' or 'groin'. At the tip of the bear's tail lies Eta Ursae Majoris, known both as Alkaid, from the Arabic meaning 'the leader', or as Benetnasch, from the Arabic meaning 'daughters of the bier' – for the Arabs regarded this figure not as a bear but as a bier or coffin. They saw the tail of the bear as a line of mourners leading the coffin.

Second in line along the tail is the wide double star Zeta Ursae Majoris. The two members of the double, visible separately with keen eyesight, are called Mizar and Alcor and were depicted as a horse and its rider on the 1524 star chart of Peter Apian. The name Mizar is a corruption of the Arabic *al-maraqq*, the same origin as the name Merak. Its companion, Alcor, gets its name from a corruption of the Arabic *al-jaun*, meaning 'the black horse or bull', the same origin as the name Alioth which is applied to the next star in the tail, Epsilon Ursae Majoris. Delta Ursae Majoris is named Megrez, from the Arabic meaning 'root of the tail'. Gamma Ursae Majoris is called Phecda, from the Arabic word meaning 'the thigh'.

In addition to the famous seven stars of Ursa Major there are three pairs of stars that mark the feet of the bear. The Arabs imagined these as forming the tracks of a leaping gazelle. The pair Nu and Xi Ursae Majoris are called Alula Borealis and Alula Australis. The word Alula is Arabic meaning 'first leap'; the distinctions 'northern' and 'southern' are added in Latin. The second leap is represented by Lambda and Mu Ursae Majoris, known as Tania Borealis and Tania Australis, while the third leap is represented by Iota and Kappa Ursae Majoris, although Iota alone bears the name Talitha.

Ursa minor
— *the little bear* —

The Little Bear was said by the Greeks to have been first named by the astronomer Thales of Miletus, who lived from about 625 BC to 545 BC. The

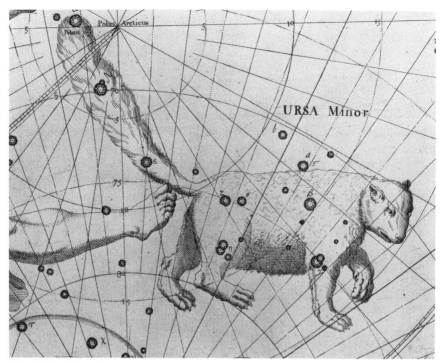

Ursa Minor from the *Atlas Coelestis* of John Flamsteed. Polaris, the north pole star, lies at the tip of its long tail.

earliest reference seems to have been made by the poet Callimachus of the third century BC, who reported that Thales 'measured out the little stars of the Wain by which the Phoenicians sail'. Certainly Homer, two centuries before Thales, wrote only of the Great Bear, never mentioning the Little Bear. However, it is not clear whether Thales actually invented the constellation or merely introduced it to the Greeks, for Thales was reputedly descended from a Phoenician family and, as Callimachus said, the Phoenicians navigated by reference to Ursa Minor rather than Ursa Major. Aratus points out that although the Little Bear is smaller and fainter than the Great Bear, it lies closer to the pole and hence provides a better guide to true north. We have the word of Eratosthenes that the Greeks also knew Ursa Minor as the Phoenician.

Aratus called the constellation Cynosura, Greek for 'dog's tail'. This is the origin of the English word cynosure, meaning 'guiding star'. According to Aratus the Little Bear represents one of the two nymphs who nursed the infant Zeus in the cave of Dicte on Crete. Apollodorus tells us that the nurses' names were Adrasteia and Ida. Ursa Minor commemorates Ida while Adrasteia, the senior of the two, is Ursa Major.

Ursa Minor has a similar ladle shape to Ursa Major, and so it is popularly termed the Little Dipper. At the end of the Little Bear's tail (or the Dipper's handle) is the star Alpha Ursae Minoris, commonly known by the Latin name Polaris because it is the north pole star. Contrary to common belief, the north pole star is not particularly bright. Polaris is a second-magnitude star, lying about a degree away from the exact north celestial pole, close enough to make it an excellent guide star for navigators.

The second star in the Little Bear's tail, Delta Ursae Minoris, is called Yildun, a mis-spelling of the Turkish word *yildiz* meaning 'star'. According to the German star-name authority Paul Kunitzsch this was wrongly thought to be a Turkish name for the pole star in Renaissance times, and it has since been arbitrarily applied to the star nearest to the true pole star.

Two stars in the bowl of the Little Dipper, Beta and Gamma Ursae Minoris, are sometimes referred to as the guardians of the pole. Their names are Kochab and Pherkad. Paul Kunitzsch has been unable to trace the origin of Kochab, but thinks that it may come from the Arabic word *kaukab* meaning 'star'. Pherkad is from the Arabic word meaning 'the two calves', referring to both Beta and Gamma Ursae Minoris.

Vela
— the sails —

One of the three sections into which the French astronomer Nicolas Louis de Lacaille divided the Greek constellation of Argo Navis, the Argonauts' ship, in 1763. Vela represents the ship's sails; the other sections are Carina, the Keel, and Puppis, the Stern. As a result of the dismantling of Argo Navis, Vela has no stars labelled Alpha or Beta, since these stars were retained in Carina. Its brightest star is Gamma Velorum, a second-magnitude double star. For mythology and an illustration, see the entry on Argo Navis in Chapter Four.

Virgo
— the virgin —

Virgo is the second-largest constellation in the sky, exceeded only by the much fainter Hydra; the Greeks called the constellation Parthenos. She is usually identified as Dike, goddess of justice, who was daughter of Zeus and Themis; but she is also known as Astraeia, daughter of Astraeus (father of the stars) and Eos (goddess of the dawn). Virgo is depicted with wings, reminiscent of an angel, holding an ear of wheat.

Dike features as the impartial observer in a moral tale depicting mankind's declining standards. It was a favourite tale of Greek and Roman mythologists, and its themes sound familiar even today.

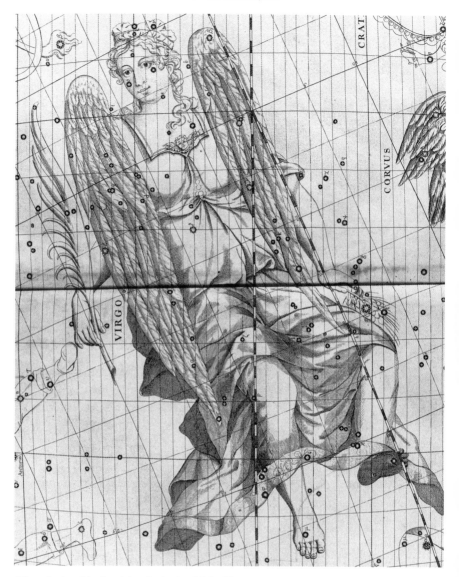

Virgo depicted in the *Atlas Coelestis* of John Flamsteed. In her right hand she carries a palm frond, while in her left hand she holds an ear of wheat marked by the bright star Spica.

Dike was supposed to have lived on Earth in the Golden Age of mankind, when Cronus ruled Olympus. It was a time of peace and happiness, a season of perennial spring when food grew without cultivation and humans never grew old. Men lived like the gods, not knowing work, sorrow, crime or war. Dike moved among them, dispensing wisdom and justice.

Then, when Zeus overthrew his father Cronus on Olympus, the Silver Age began, inferior to the age that had just passed. In the Silver Age, Zeus shortened springtime and introduced the yearly cycle of seasons. Humans in this age became quarrelsome and ceased to honour the gods. Dike longed for the idyllic days gone by. She assembled the human race and spoke sternly to them for forsaking the ideals of their ancestors. 'Worse is to come', she warned them. Then she spread her wings and took refuge in the mountains, turning her back on mankind. Finally came the Ages of Bronze and Iron, when humans descended into violence, theft and war. Unable to bear the sins of humanity any longer, Dike abandoned the Earth and flew up to heaven, where she sits to this day next to the constellation of Libra, which some see as the scales of justice.

There are other goddesses who can claim identity with Virgo. One is Demeter, the corn goddess, who was daughter of Cronus and Rhea. By her brother Zeus she had a daughter, Persephone (also called Kore, meaning 'maiden'). Persephone might have remained a virgin for ever had not her uncle, Hades, god of the Underworld, kidnapped her while she was out picking flowers one day at Henna in Sicily. Hades swept her aboard his chariot drawn by four black horses and galloped with her into his underground kingdom, where she became his reluctant queen.

Demeter, having scoured the Earth for her missing daughter without success, cursed the fields of Sicily so that the crops failed. In desperation she asked the Great Bear what he had seen, since he never sets, but since the abduction had taken place during the day he referred her to the Sun, who finally told her the truth.

Demeter angrily confronted Zeus, father of Persephone, and demanded that he order his brother Hades to return the girl. Zeus agreed to try; but already it was too late, because Persephone had eaten some pomegranate seeds while in the Underworld, and once having done that she could never return permanently to the land of the living. A compromise was reached in which Persephone would spend half (some say one-third) of the year in the Underworld with her husband, and the rest of the year above ground with her mother. Clearly, this is an allegory on the changing seasons.

Eratosthenes offers the additional suggestion that Virgo might be Atargatis, the Syrian fertility goddess, who was sometimes depicted holding an ear of corn. But Atargatis is identified with the constellation Piscis Austrinus (q.v.). Hyginus identifies Virgo with Erigone, the daughter of Icarius, who hanged herself after the death of her father. In this story, Icarius became the constellation Boötes, which adjoins Virgo to the north, and Icarius's dog Maera became the star Procyon (see Boötes and Canis Minor).

Eratosthenes and Hyginus both name Tyche, the goddess of fortune, as another identification of Virgo; but Tyche was usually represented holding the horn of plenty (cornucopia) rather than an ear of grain. In the sky, the ear of corn is represented by the first-magnitude star Spica, Latin for 'ear of grain' (the name in Greek, Stachos, has the same meaning).

Beta Virginis is called Zavijava, from an Arabic name meaning 'the angle'. Gamma Virginis is named Porrima, after a Roman goddess. According to Ovid in his *Fasti*, Porrima and her sister Postverta were the sisters or companions of the prophetess Carmenta. Porrima sang of events in the past, while Postverta sang of what was to come.

Epsilon Virginis is named Vindemiatrix, from the Latin meaning 'grape-gatherer' or 'vintager', because its first visible rising before the Sun in August marked the beginning of each year's vintage. Ovid in his *Fasti* tells us that this star commemorates a boy named Ampelus (the Greek word for 'vine') who was loved by Dionysus, god of wine. While picking grapes from a vine that trailed up an elm tree, Ampelus fell from a branch and was killed; Dionysus placed him among the stars. This star's Greek name, Protrygeter, also means 'grape gatherer'. Its importance as a calendar star is shown by the fact that it was one of the few stars named by Aratus and, at third magnitude, was far fainter than the others. Vindemiatrix marks the top of Virgo's right wing.

Volans
— *the flying fish* —

One of the twelve new constellations introduced at the end of the sixteenth century by the Dutch navigators Pieter Dirkszoon Keyser and Frederick de Houtman. Volans represents a real type of fish found in tropical waters that can leap out of the water and glide through the air on wings. The constellation was first depicted in 1598 on a globe by the Dutchman Petrus Plancius. The constellation was originally known by the name of Piscis Volans. Its brightest stars are of only fourth magnitude, none are named and there are no legends associated with the constellation.

Volans shown under the name Piscis Volans in the *Uranographia* of Johann Bode.

Vulpecula
— *the fox* —

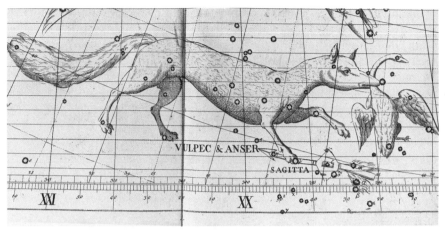

Vulpecula was originally known as the fox and goose, Vulpecula and Anser, as on this illustration from the *Atlas Coelestis* of John Flamsteed.

A constellation introduced in 1687 by the Polish astronomer Johannes Hevelius, who depicted it as a double figure of a fox, Vulpecula, carrying in its jaws a goose, Anser. Since then the goose has flown (or been eaten), leaving just the fox. Hevelius is said to have placed the fox near two other hunting animals, the eagle (the constellation Aquila) and the vulture (an alternative identification of Lyra). Vulpecula contains no named stars and has no legends. Although its brightest stars are of only fourth magnitude it is notable for the Dumb-bell Nebula, reputedly the most conspicuous of the class of so-called planetary nebulae. The Dumb-bell Nebula consists of gas thrown off from a dying star; it takes its name from the double-lobed structure, like a bar-bell, as seen on long-exposure photographs.

— *Milky way* —

The Milky Way is not, of course, a constellation, but is a band of faint light crossing the sky; the Roman writer Manilius compared it to the luminous wake of a ship. Ovid in his *Metamorphoses* described it as a road lined either side by the houses of distinguished gods – 'the Palatine district of high heaven', he termed it. Along this road the gods supposedly travelled to the palace of Zeus.

Eratosthenes tells us that the Milky Way was the result of a trick played by Zeus on his wife Hera so that she would suckle his illegitimate son

Heracles and hence make him immortal. Hermes laid the infant Heracles at Hera's breast while she was asleep, but when she woke and realized who the baby was – perhaps by the strength with which he sucked – she pushed him away and her milk squirted across the sky to form the Milky Way.

Manilius listed various explanations for the Milky Way that were current in his day, both scientific and mythological. One suggestion was that it is the seam where the two halves of the heavens are joined – or, conversely, where the two halves are coming apart like a split in the ceiling, letting in light from beyond. Alternatively, says Manilius, it might be a former path of the Sun, now covered in ash where the sky was scorched. Some thought that it could mark the route taken by Phaethon when he careered across the sky in the chariot of the Sun god, Helios, setting the sky on fire (see Eridanus). Yet again it could be a mass of faint stars, an idea attributed to the Greek philosopher Democritus of the fifth century BC, which we now know to be correct. Finally, Manilius suggests that the Milky Way could be the abode of the souls of heroes who have ascended to heaven.

—*Obsolete constellations*—

NON-ASTRONOMERS ARE OFTEN PUZZLED BY THE IDEA OF A DISUSED CONSTELLATION – SURELY, A CONSTELLATION IS EITHER there or it isn't. However, the patterns we see in the stars are purely a product of human imagination, so humans are free to amend the patterns as they choose – and astronomers did so during the heyday of celestial mapping in the seventeenth and eighteenth centuries.

The constellations described in this section are a selection of those that, for one reason or another, are no longer recognized by astronomers, although they will be found on old maps. I have described only those constellations that achieved at least some degree of currency, for constellations invented by one astronomer, either to make his own name or to flatter his patrons, could be introduced at will and be completely ignored by everyone else. For example, in 1754 the English naturalist John Hill invented thirteen new constellations, tucked into spaces between existing figures, representing various unappealing animals including a toad (Bufo), a leech (Hirudo), a spider (Aranea), an earthworm (Lumbricus), and a slug (Limax). Hill was a noted satirist, and he may have been attemping to perpetrate a joke on astronomers – a joke that never caught on.

Several constellations were introduced for mercenary reasons, by astronomers wishing to immortalize their kings or governments, usually in the hope that such a gesture would advance their career, as it often did. A German astronomer, Julius Schiller of Augsburg, attempted to populate the sky entirely with Biblical characters – for example, the familiar constellations of the zodiac were changed to represent the twelve apostles. These attempts to politicize and Christianize the sky were rejected by other astronomers.

— *Antinous* —

Antinous was the boy lover of the Roman Emperor Hadrian and hence is a real character, not a mythological one, although the story reads like fiction. Antinous was born *c.*AD 110 in the town of Bythinium, near present-day Bolu in north-western Turkey. At that time this area was a Roman province, which is how he came to meet the Emperor. While on a trip up the Nile with Hadrian in AD 130, Antinous drowned near the present-day town of Mallawi in Egypt. Supposedly an oracle had predicted that the Emperor would be saved from danger by the sacrifice of the object he most loved, and Antinous realized that this description applied to him. Whether the drowning was accident or suicide, Hadrian was heartbroken by it. He founded a city called Antinopolis near the site of the boy's death and commemorated him in the sky from stars south of Aquila, the Eagle, that had not previously been considered part of any constellation. The constellation Antinous was mentioned as a sub-division of Aquila by Ptolemy in his *Almagest* (which was written about twenty years after the famous drowning), and it was first depicted in 1551 on a star globe by Gerardus Mercator. Tycho Brahe listed it as a separate constellation in 1602. Antinous was depicted being carried in the claws of Aquila. Hence he has sometimes been confused with Ganymede, another celestial catamite, who was carried off by an eagle for Zeus.

Antinous seen in the claws of Aquila in the *Uranographia* of Johann Bode.

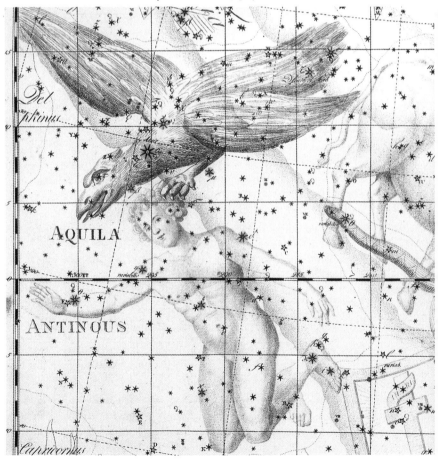

Argo navis
— *the ship argo* —

Argo is a constellation that is not so much disused as dismantled. It was one of the forty-eight constellations known to Greek astronomers, as listed by Ptolemy, but astronomers in the eighteenth century found it large and unwieldy and so divided it into three parts, Carina, the Keel, Puppis, the Poop (i.e. stern), and Vela, the Sails.

Argo Navis represents the fifty-oared galley in which Jason and the Argonauts sailed to fetch the golden fleece from Colchis in the Black Sea. Jason entrusted the building of the ship to Argus, after whom it was named. Argus built the ship under the orders of the goddess Athene at the port of Pagasae, using timber from nearby Mount Pelion. Into the prow Athene fitted an oak beam from the oracle of Zeus at Dodona in north-western Greece. This area, like the island of Corfu nearby, was once noted for its forests of oak, before later shipbuilders stripped them bare. Being part of an

Argo Navis in the *Uranographia* of Johann Bode. Only the stern of the ship is depicted in the sky. On the blade of one of the steering oars lies the bright star Canopus.

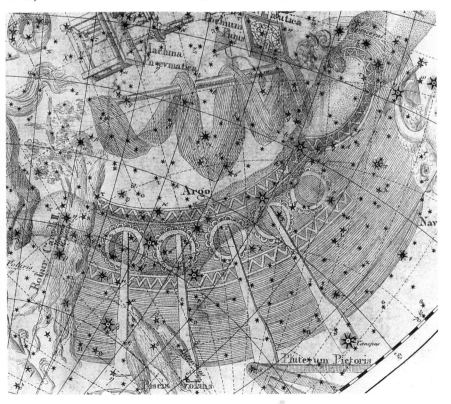

oracle, this oak beam could speak and it was crying out for action by the time the Argo left harbour.

Jason took with him fifty of the greatest Greek heroes, including the twins Castor and Polydeuces, the musician Orpheus and Argus, the ship's builder. Even Heracles interrupted his labours to join the crew.

Apollonius of Rhodes, who wrote the epic story of the ship's voyage to Colchis and back, described Argo as the finest ship that ever braved the sea with oars. Even in the roughest of seas the bolts of Argo held her planks together safely, and she ran as sweetly when the crew were pulling at the oars as she did before the wind. Isaac Newton thought the voyage of the Argo was commemorated in the twelve signs of the zodiac, although the connections are hard to see.

Among the greatest dangers the Argonauts faced en route were the Clashing Rocks, or Symplegades, which guarded the entrance to the Black Sea like a pair of sliding doors, crushing ships between them. As the Argonauts rowed along the Bosphorus, they could hear the terrifying clash of the Rocks and the thunder of surf. The Argonauts released a dove and watched it fly ahead of them. The Rocks converged on the dove, nipping off its tail feathers, but the bird got through. Then, as the Rocks separated, the Argonauts rowed with all their might. A well-timed push from the divine hand of Athene helped the ship through the Rocks just as they slammed together again, shearing off the mascot from Argo's stern. Argo had become the first ship to run the gauntlet of the Rocks and survive. Thereafter the Clashing Rocks remained rooted apart.

Once safely into the Black Sea, Jason and the Argonauts headed for Colchis. There they stole the golden fleece from King Aeetes, and made off with it back to Greece by a roundabout route. After their return, Jason left the Argo beached at Corinth, where he dedicated it to Poseidon, the sea god.

Eratosthenes said that the constellation represents the first ocean-going ship ever built, and the Roman writer Manilius concurred. However the first ship was actually built by Danaus, father of the fifty Danaids, again with the help of Athene, and he sailed in it with his daughters from Libya to Argos.

Only the stern of Argo is shown in the sky. Map makers attempted to account for this either by depicting its prow vanishing into a bank of mist, as Aratus described it, or by passing between the Clashing Rocks. Robert Graves recounts the explanation that Jason in his old age returned to Corinth where he sat beneath the rotting hulk of Argo, contemplating past events. Just at that moment the rotten beams of the prow fell off and killed him. Poseidon then placed the rest of the ship among the stars. Hyginus, though, says that Athene placed Argo among the stars from steering oars to sail when the ship was first launched, but says nothing about what happened to the prow.

Argo was first divided into three parts by the French astronomer Nicolas Louis de Lacaille in his catalogue of the southern stars published in 1763 and it now lies permanently dismembered.

— *Cerberus* —

A constellation representing the three-headed monster that guarded Hades. It is depicted being held in the outstretched hand of Hercules, who tamed the dog as one of his labours. The constellation was introduced by Johannes Hevelius on his map of 1687, replacing the branch from the tree of the golden apples that had previously been depicted in the hand of Hercules. Although Cerberus was supposed to be a dog in mythology, Hevelius and all subsequent map makers represented it as three snake heads. The English engraver John Senex, a friend of Edmond Halley, combined Cerberus with the apple branch, Ramus, in 1721 to produce Cerberus et Ramus, the serpents being wrapped around the branch.

Cerberus et Ramus shown in the *Uranographia* of Johann Bode.

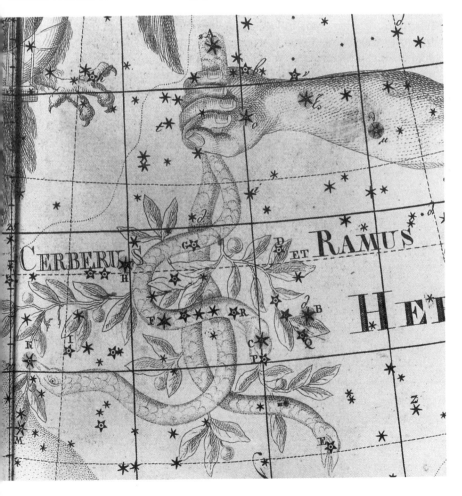

Custos messium
— *the harvest keeper* —

Introduced by the French astronomer Joseph-Jerome de Lalande on his celestial globe of 1779. The name Custos Messium is a punning reference to his countryman Charles Messier, and in fact the constellation was often known as Messier. It lay between Cassiopeia and the north celestial pole, next to another now-abandoned constellation, Rangifer the Reindeer. For illustration, see Camelopardalis.

Felis
— *the cat* —

Invented at the end of the eighteenth century by the Frenchman Joseph-Jerome de Lalande because, he said, 'I am very fond of cats.' It was made from stars between Antlia and Hydra. Lalande did not himself depict the constellation on any globe or chart; it was first shown on Bode's atlas of 1801.

A grumpy-looking Felis on the *Uranographia* of Johann Bode.

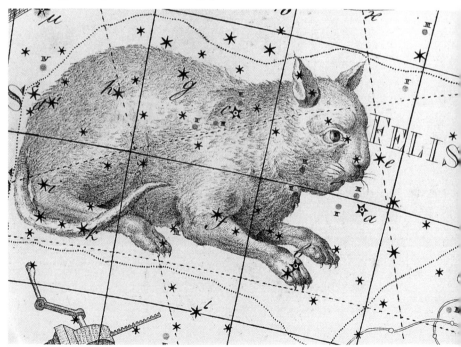

Gallus
— the cockerel —

Petrus Plancius, a Dutch theologian, formed this constellation in 1613 to represent the cockerel that crowed for the second time after Peter had denied Jesus thrice. It lay in the Milky Way, in the northern part of what is now Puppis. Although a number of astronomers adopted Gallus, it was not shown on the influential charts of Johann Bode.

Globus aerostaticus
— the balloon —

This constellation first appeared on the atlas of Johann Elert Bode in 1801, but it was suggested by Joseph-Jerome de Lalande in honour of the Montgolfier brothers, pioneer balloonists. It lay south of Aquarius and Capricornus. For illustration, see Capricornus.

Harpa georgii
— George's Harp —

Harpa Georgii in the *Uranographia* of Johann Bode.

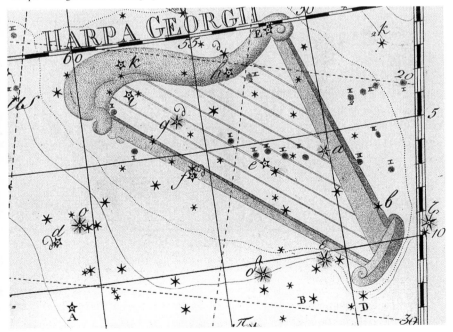

Maximilian Hell, an Austrian Jesuit astronomer, introduced this constellation in 1789 from stars beneath the feet of Taurus. He used the name Psalterium Georgianum. It honours King George III of England, patron of William Herschel, the discoverer of Uranus. Both Herschel and King George were of German extraction. Bode changed the name to Harpa Georgii on his atlas of 1801.

Honores friderici
— Frederick's Glories —

A constellation introduced by Johann Bode in 1787 to commemorate King Frederick the Great of Prussia, who had died the preceding year. Bode originally called it by the German name of Friedrichs Ehre, but Latinized the name on his atlas of 1801. The constellation was squeezed in next to Lacerta, the Lizard. In this same area the Frenchman Augustin Royer had in 1679 placed his own invention, Sceptrum, representing the French sceptre and hand of justice, commemorating Louis XIV.

— Jordanus —

A constellation representing the river Jordan, introduced by the Dutchman Petrus Plancius on his celestial globe of 1613. Jordan had its source near the tail of the Great Bear in what is now the constellation of Canes Venatici, flowed under the Bear's feet and ended near the head of the Bear in Camelopardalis, another Plancius invention. Jordanus was not shown by Bode.

Lochium funis
— the log and line —

An addition to the constellation Argo, introduced by Bode on his 1801 atlas, representing a nautical log and line used for measuring distance travelled at sea. It was positioned next to Pyxis, the Compass. For illustration, see Pyxis.

Machina electrica
— the electrical machine —

A constellation introduced by Bode on his atlas of 1801, representing one of the mechanical wonders of the age, an electrostatic generator. It lay in the southern hemisphere, between the modern Fornax and Sculptor.

Machina Electrica, a constellation invented by Johann Bode and shown in his *Uranographia.*

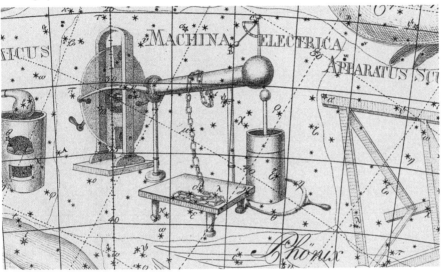

Mons maenalus
— mount maenalus —

A mountain of Arcadia in the central Peloponnese, introduced as a constellation by Johannes Hevelius in his star atlas of 1687, where he depicted it as a mountain on which Boötes is standing. It appeared on many later maps, always as part of Boötes, and it never had an independent existence. For illustration, see Boötes.

Musca borealis
— the northern fly —

This constellation has a confusing history. It was introduced on a globe of 1613 attributed to the Dutchman Petrus Plancius. He called it Apes, the Bee, and it lay just north of Aries. The German astronomer Jacob Bartsch changed the name to Vespa, the Wasp, on his map of 1624. Johannes

Hevelius renamed it Musca on his atlas of 1687. But there was already an equivalent insect in the southern sky, and so the northern fly was eventually swatted by astronomers. To add to the confusion, the same stars were used in 1674 by the Frenchman Ignace-Gaston Pardies to form Lilium, the fleur-de-lis of France.

Musca borealis crawls across a chart from the *Uranographia* of Johann Bode.

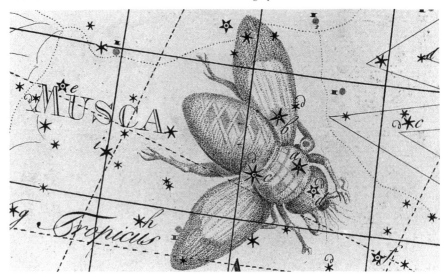

Officina typographica
— *the printing shop* —

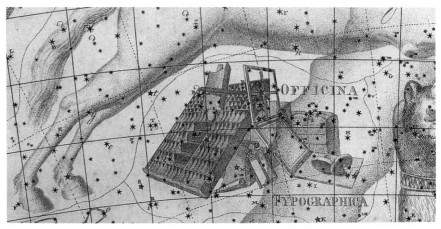

Officina Typographica, invented by Johann Bode and shown in his *Uranographia*.

Johann Bode introduced this constellation in 1801 to commemorate the 350th anniversary of Gutenberg's invention of printing with movable type. It lay in what is now the northern part of Puppis, the stern of the ship Argo.

Quadrans muralis
— the mural quadrant —

One of the best-known of the abandoned constellations, because it has given its name to the annual meteor shower known as the Quadrantids that radiates from this area every Janaury. The constellation was invented by Joseph-Jerome de Lalande to commemorate the wall-mounted instrument which he used for measuring star positions. It was first pictured on the 1795 atlas of J. Fortin, another Frenchman. Quadrans Muralis occupied what is now the northern part of Boötes, near the tip of the Plough's handle. For illustration, see Boötes.

Rangifer
— the reindeer —

Introduced by the Frenchman Pierre-Charles Le Monnier on his star map of 1743, under the name le Renne. Fittingly, the celestial reindeer was placed near the north pole of the sky. Le Monnier invented the constellation after his trip to Lapland to measure the length of a degree of latitude in the far north. It has also been known under the name of Tarandus. For illustration, see Camelopardalis.

Robur carolinum
— Charles's Oak —

A constellation devised by Edmond Halley in 1678 as a patriotic gesture to King Charles II. It commemorates the oak in which the King hid after his defeat by Oliver Cromwell's republican forces at the Battle of Worcester. Halley formed the constellation out of stars that were previously part of Argo Navis when he returned from a visit to St Helena during which he had mapped the southern skies. The constellation was rejected by the French astronomer Nicolas Louis de Lacaille, who mapped the southern skies seventy-five years after Halley, but Bode showed it on his atlas of 1801 as Robur Caroli II.

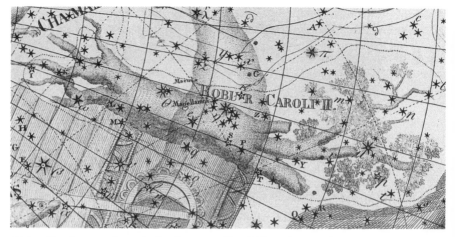

Robur Carolinum as shown in the *Uranographia* of Johann Bode.

Sceptrum brandenburgicum
— *the Brandenburg sceptre* —

Introduced in 1688 by the German astronomer Godfried Kirch to honour the Brandenburg province of Prussia in which he lived. Its stars are now part of Eridanus.

Sceptrum Brandenburgicum from the *Uranographia* of Johann Bode.

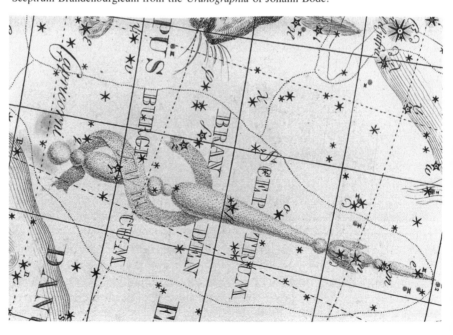

Taurus poniatovii
— *Poniatowski's bull* —

This constellation was originated in 1777 by Martin Poczobut, director of the Royal Observatory at Vilna, to honour his king, Stanislas II of Poland. It was first depicted by the Frenchman Lalande on his celestial globe of 1779. It was made from a V-shaped group of stars that Ptolemy in his *Almagest* had classified as being outside Ophiuchus. Poczobut thought that this group resembled the Hyades cluster that forms the face of Taurus in the zodiac. It is now part of Ophiuchus.

Taurus poniatovii depicted on the *Uranographia* of Johann Bode.

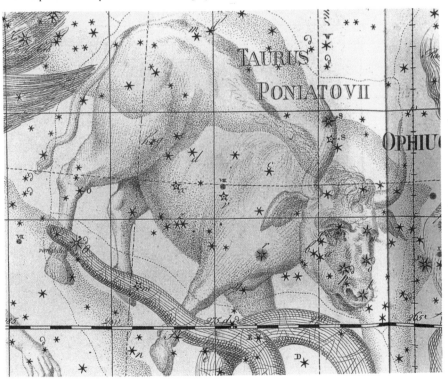

Telescopium herschelii
— *Herschel's telescope* —

There were originally two such constellations, invented in 1789 by Maximilian Hell of Vienna to commemorate William Herschel's discovery of the planet Uranus. The two constellations flanked the area in which the new planet was found. Tubus Herschelii Major, as Hell called it, represented Herschel's 20 ft (6 m) long telescope, and lay between Gemini and Auriga. Tubus Herschelii Minor, crammed awkwardly between Orion and Taurus, represented Herschel's 7 ft (2 m) reflector. Bode reduced the constellations to one, depicting the 7 ft telescope with which Herschel actually discovered Uranus where Hell had placed Tubus Herschelii Major.

Telescopium herschelii, a reflecting telescope, shown on the *Uranographia* of Johann Bode.

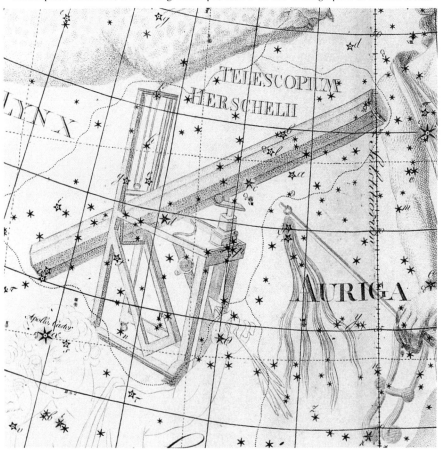

— *Tigris* —

A constellation representing the river Tigris, introduced in 1613 by the Dutchman Petrus Plancius on the same globe as the river Jordan made its first appearance. Tigris began in Ophiuchus and flowed between Cygnus and Aquila, ending at Pegasus. It was not shown by Johann Bode.

Triangulum minor
— the little triangle —

One of the least imaginative constellations, invented by Johannes Hevelius in 1687. It was formed from three stars adjacent to the existing triangle, Triangulum. It achieved surprisingly wide acceptance among astronomers, but ultimately was doomed to oblivion when the constellations came to be rationalized. For illustration, see Triangulum.

Turdus solitarius
— the solitaire —

This perplexing constellation was introduced in 1776 by the French astronomer Pierre-Charles Le Monnier under the name of the Solitaire, supposedly representing an extinct flightless bird similar to the Dodo that was formerly found on the island of Rodrigues in the Indian Ocean. But the solitaire shown on Le Monnier's chart of the constellation was a rock thrush (genus Turdus) known as the solitaire of the Philippines. To confuse matters further, the British scientist Thomas Young renamed the constellation the Mocking Bird on his star map of 1806, and on still other maps it was changed into Noctua, the Night Owl. Before it became as extinct as the bird after which it was originally named, the constellation occupied an area at the tip of the Hydra's tail.

Turdus Solitarius from the *Uranographia* of Johann Bode.

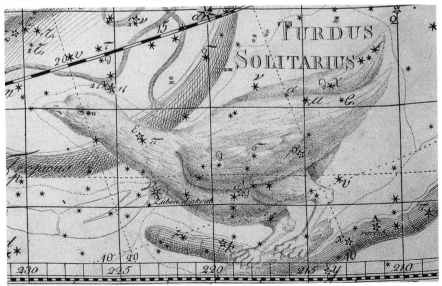

—*Glossary*—

The Greeks and Romans had similar gods and mythological characters, but used different names for them. Hence what may sound at first to be two different characters, such as Zeus and Jupiter, are really one and the same. The following list gives the *Latin* equivalents of the major Greek characters mentioned in this book.

Aphrodite	*Venus*	Hephaestus	*Vulcan*
Ares	*Mars*	Hermes	*Mercury*
Artemis	*Diana*	Hera	*Juno*
Asclepius	*Aesculapius*	Heracles	*Hercules*
Athene	*Minerva*	Hades	*Pluto*
Cronos	*Saturn*	Persephone	*Proserpina*
Demeter	*Ceres*	Polydeuces	*Pollux*
Dionysus	*Bacchus*	Poseidon	*Neptune*
Eros	*Cupid*	Zeus	*Jupiter*

—Sources and references—

For anyone entering the field of Greek mythology, the two volumes by Robert Graves entitled *The Greek Myths* (Penguin) are a masterful synthesis, with copious references. Another useful summary, with many notes and references, is *A Handbook of Greek Mythology* by H.J. Rose (Methuen). For other background information I consulted the *Oxford Classical Dictionary* (Oxford University Press) and the *Dictionary of Classical Mythology* by Pierre Grimal (Blackwell); the latter, in particular, contains a fund of references.

The starting point for all studies of Greek star lore is a poem called the *Phaenomena (Appearances)*, written *c.*275 BC by Aratus of Soli. The *Phaenomena* of Aratus is based on a book of the same name written the previous century by the Greek scientist Eudoxus of Cnidus. No copies of the book by Eudoxus have been preserved; we only have Aratus's poem. Aratus has been translated into English by G.R. Mair in the Loeb Classical Library series (Harvard University Press and Heinemann).

The Latin adaptation of Aratus that was reputedly written by Germanicus Caesar in the early part of the first century has been translated by D.B. Gain; see *The Aratus Ascribed to Germanicus Caesar* (Athlone Press, 1976). A Latin work with many echoes of Aratus is *Astronomica* by the Roman poet Marcus Manilius, written early in the first century AD. It has been translated into English by G.P. Goold in the Loeb Classical Library.

Another early Greek source is the *Catasterisms* ascribed to Eratosthenes in the second century BC (though not, according to modern authority, actually written by him). This is a highly obscure essay and I could find no record of an English translation. I referred to the French version of the *Catasterisms* published in 1821 by Abbé Halma.

The Myths of Hyginus by Mary Grant (University of Kansas Publications, 1960) contains an invaluable English translation of Hyginus's *Fabulae* and *Poetica Astronomica*, among the most influential works on constellation mythology but scarcely read today.

Apollodorus was a Greek writer who produced an encyclopedic summary of Greek myths called the Library; I referred to the Loeb translation by Sir J.G. Frazer. Many popular myths received their definitive retelling in the works of the Roman writer Ovid; for his *Metamorphoses*, I used the Penguin translation by Mary Innes, and the Loeb edition of his *Fasti* by Sir J.G. Frazer. My source for Apollonius Rhodius was the Penguin translation by E.V. Rieu. For Ptolemy's *Almagest*, I consulted G.J. Toomer's thoughtful translation (Duckworth, 1984).

For the origin of star names, I have relied on the booklet *Short Guide to Modern Star Names and Their Derivations* by Paul Kunitzsch and Tim Smart (Otto Harrassowitz, Wiesbaden, 1986). Useful background on star names can also be found in an article by Dr Kunitzsch in the January 1983 issue of *Sky & Telescope*. An illuminating paper by Gwyneth Heuter on the origin of star names is to be found in *Vistas in Astronomy*, vol. 29, 1986, p. 237.

The Sky Explored by Deborah J. Warner (Alan R. Liss, New York, and Theatrum Orbis Terrarum, Netherlands) is an invaluable survey of the history and development of celestial cartography, and contains much incidental material on constellation history.

Archie Roy's speculations about the origin of the constellations are contained in his paper in *Vistas in Astronomy*, vol. 27, 1984, p.171. E.R. Knobel's analysis of the star catalogue of Frederick de Houtman is in the *Monthly Notices of the Royal Astronomical Society*, vol. 77, 1917, p. 414.

R.H. Allen's *Star Names, Their Lore and Meaning* (Dover) and W.T. Olcott's *Star Lore of All Ages* (Putnam's) are fun to dip into, but I have not used them as prime sources for mythology.

—Index—
to Stars and Constellations

—*Acknowledgements*—

The author and Publisher would like to thank the following for their kind permission to reproduce the following illustrations from their collections:

Albrecht Dürer, The National Maritime Museum, London: 4, 5.

Délimitation Scientifique des Constellations, Eugene Delporte, Royal Astronomical Society Library, London: 12.

Tunhuang mss (MS Stein 3326) By permission of the British Library: 14.

Book of the Fixed Stars (MS Marsh 144, p. 111) By permission of the Bodleian Library: 15.

Uranometria, Johann Bayer, Institute of Astronomy Library, University of Cambridge: 16.

Firmamentum Sobiescianum, Johannes Hevelius, Institute of Astronomy Library, University of Cambridge: 18.

Uranographia, Johann Bode, The Royal Observatory: 22, 23, 24, 28, 32, 34, 36, 37, 38, 41, 42, 44, 48, 52, 53, 54, 55, 57, 58, 63, 64, 67, 71, 76, 79, 80, 82, 85, 86, 88, 90, 92, 93, 97, 100, 101, 103, 106, 109, 110, 111, 113, 115, 116, 117, 123, 125, 127, 134, 138, 139, 141, 142, 143, 145, 146, 148, 149, 150, 151.

Atlas Coelestis, John Flamsteed, The Royal Observatory: 25, 27, 30, 39, 46, 49, 51, 56, 59, 62, 69, 73, 77, 81, 83, 84, 91, 94, 107, 111, 118, 119, 124, 130, 135.